STRAT… …R'S

M… …TE

HOW TO USE M… …RLITE TO BUILD AN AUTHOR NEWSLETTER

STRATEGIC AUTHOR SERIES BOOK 1

ERIKA EVEREST

eddally
PUBLISHING

First Edition published August 2020 (v1.0)

ISBN: 978-1-913972-00-4

The author is not affiliated with MailerLite or BookFunnel (she just really loves both products!)

Dedication

To everyone in the 20BooksTo50K® Community,

Michael Anderle, for founding it,

and Craig Martelle, for leading it,

THANK YOU.

Beta Testing Team and Jitterbugs

Fatima Bader

Julian Barr

Elaine Bateman

James Caplan

Kasia Lasinska

Anne Lown

Robyn Sarty

Contents

1. Introduction

If you are reading this, I assume that you've already decided that you want or need a newsletter – and for more than just letting the world know when your new release is available. Perhaps you've read *Newsletter Ninja* by Tammi Labrecque. Perhaps you've heard bestselling author Mark Dawson say that his newsletter is his single greatest advertising tool.

Whatever it is, you know you need a newsletter.

While you may know *why* you should have a newsletter and *what* you can gain by doing it properly, you may be struggling to work out *how* to implement the strategies suggested in the sources above. I was. That's where this book comes in. I'll show you how to implement onboarding sequences, reader funnels, automation, and simple email branding set-up, step-by-step with pictures in the popular system **MailerLite**.

"Why MailerLite?" you may ask. When I was starting out with newsletters, I asked friends who were more established in their author careers what they use. The resounding answer I got at the time was MailerLite, so that's what I started with.

I made mistakes along the way. I set things up thinking I was following the advice from *Newsletter Ninja* and other sources, but I was actually making my life more difficult. That experience inspired me to create this guide to go through step-by-step how to do it right from the start, to give *you* the best chance of an effective mailing list in MailerLite.

So, whether you have many books released or are not yet published, whether you've tried mailing lists before or if you're starting from scratch, I hope you'll find this book a useful guide to getting the most out of your newsletter and achieving its full potential as your best advertising platform.

2. Getting started

Chapter Objectives

- *Setting up the pre-requisites – company address, custom domain website, and custom email.*
- *Using them to open a MailerLite account and get it approved.*
- *Exploring the MailerLite interface.*
- *Creating an author brand image.*

2.1. Registering a MailerLite account

The first step is to set up an account with MailerLite. Go to www.mailerlite.com to sign up. The Company or Organization field is your author name – the name you want your emails to come from. The email address is whatever account you want MailerLite to communicate with YOU through – this is *not* the email that you will use to contact your subscribers. Set your password and create an account.

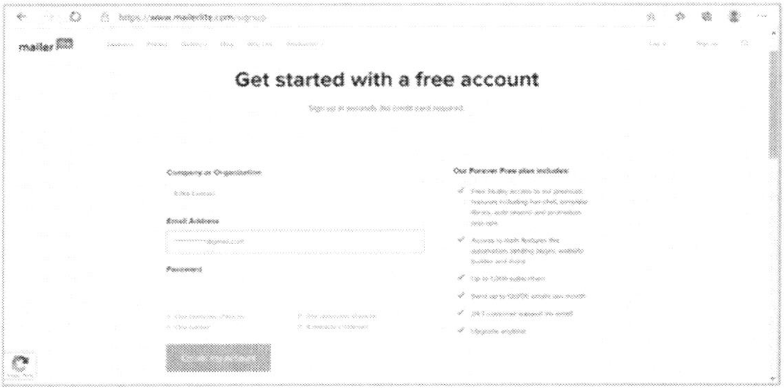

You start with a free account, and will only need to upgrade if your list size exceeds the free limit (1,000 active subscribers). You can work out what the cost will be for your list size by entering the details on mailerlite.com/pricing. The prices shown below are monthly, and there is a 30% discount on the yearly price if you pay annually in advance instead (information correct as of July 2020, though may be subject to change.)

But before you worry about upgrading or prices, you need to finish setting up your profile. When you click "Create new account" you will be brought to the Welcome page within MailerLite.

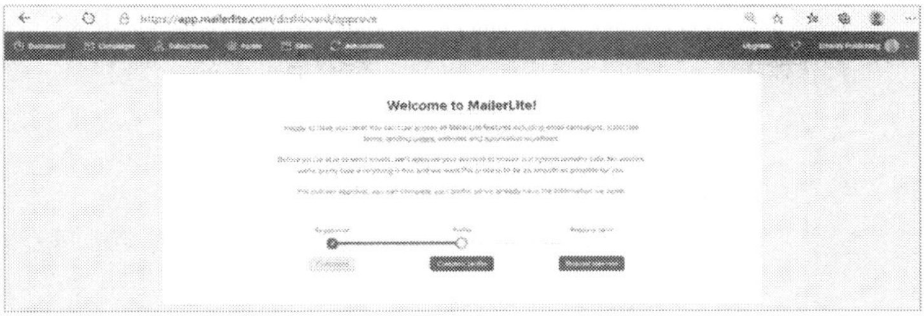

By submitting your sign-up details, you completed the first step, **Registration**. But before you can send emails, your account needs to be approved by the MailerLite team. **Request approval** is the third step in this chain, but to make that approval process quicker and easier, you should complete step 2, **Complete profile**, before requesting approval.

To complete your profile, you'll be asked to enter your personal details: your name, obviously (or at least the name from whom the emails are coming), and your address. This address is your corporate address, your business address.

To request approval, you need a website at a custom domain and a custom email address associated with this domain.

The next sections look at how to set up a custom email and company address, and how to enter this information into your MailerLite profile.

2.2. Complete profile

Your **Company or organizational name** will be pre-populated on your profile as the name you submitted during the registration step. All other profile information needs to be entered manually. Some additional profile questions not visible here include your Industry (and "author" is one of the options, so that's simple!), current mailing size (zero is an option) and prior experience with mailing list providers, how you (plan to) collect subscribers, and what content you plan to share using MailerLite's platform.

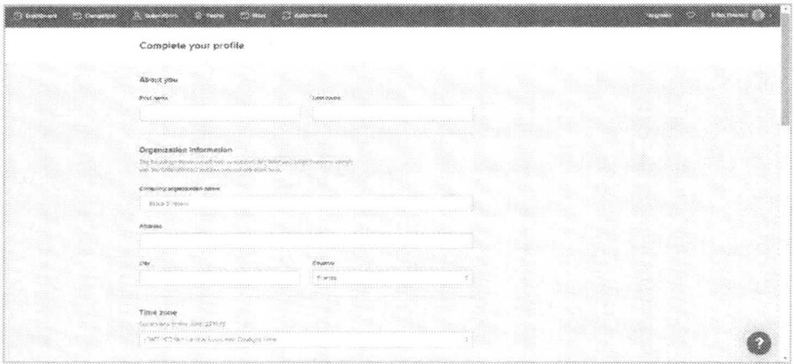

However, the address may be the hardest question to answer, despite seeming simple. This is because your organization address should appear at the bottom of every email you send. If you are self-published, you may not have a business address, so you need to decide what information you are willing to share here.

2.2.1. Company address

If you wish to keep your personal postal address private, you can choose to nominate someone else as the address for your organization. For example, maybe your accountant or someone else who can receive postal mail on your behalf. (Of course, you need the agreement of these people to act as your post-box, which they may not be willing to do, or which may incur a charge.)

Another option is to have a PO Box or other remote access service. In the US, I've been told the rates in different post offices can often be greatly different depending on the size of the town and area that post office serves. However, this may not make a difference to you, as you need a location that is easily accessible to you. But even in the same town, there can be commercial alternatives to a PO Box from USPS, that may be more affordable for the service you need.

Note that in certain jurisdictions a PO Box is not considered a company registration address and would not be permitted for this. You should check your local regulations to make sure what you choose to list as your address is appropriate for your jurisdiction.

The CAN-SPAM Act (2003) is a US law prohibiting spamming via email. (CAN-SPAM stands for Controlling the Assault of Non-Solicited Pornography and Marketing.) Among obvious rules like being truthful in the name of the sender, that the subject line accurately reflects the content, and that an opt-out/unsubscribe mechanism is provided, it requires that the sender provide a valid physical address. CAN-SPAM applies to all US people/businesses, or any company working on their behalf (i.e. you can't get your friend in Canada to run your mailing list for you to avoid needing to comply).

In Europe, the European e-Privacy Directive (ePD 2002, updated 2009) includes a requirement for "a valid address to which the recipient may send a request." The ePD applies to all emails with senders or recipients in the EU.

Thus, having a valid postal address is required for sending emails to a large proportion of English-speaking readers. Given that fines for non-compliance can be hefty, decide what information you are willing to share publicly in the footer of all your emails, and set that address up for your author business.

2.3. Request Approval

To assess whether your business meets MailerLite's terms of service, they ask to review your business website. To verify that the website you enter is indeed yours, you will be asked (in the next step) to provide an email address at the same custom domain name as your website.

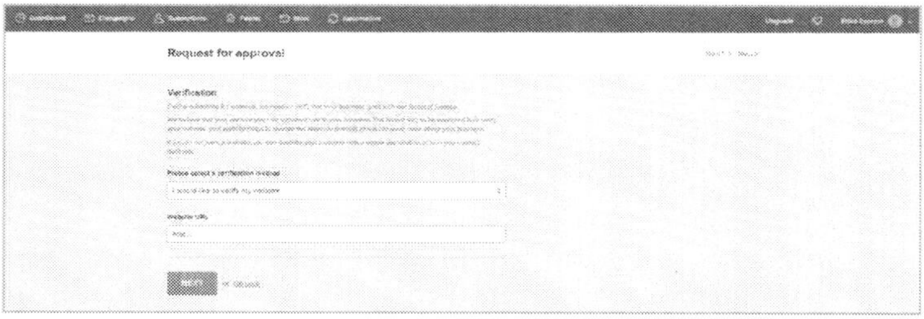

MailerLite will then send an email to this custom address and ask you to respond – this confirms that the web domain is indeed yours to use. This is important because not all website packages come with custom emails as part of them. Make sure you check for that when you're choosing your web package because you're going to need at least one custom email.

If you *don't* have a website, you can still request approval. You will need to provide a social media profile link, so MailerLite can see who you are, and a description of your business. It is important to note that in the "Tell us about your business" section, they also ask you to explain why you do not have a website for your business.

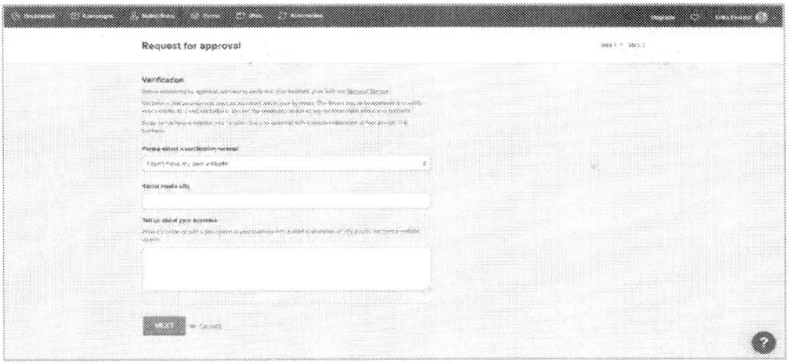

Not having a website will slow down the approval process, and may lead to your application being subject to additional scrutiny or possibly rejected. Furthermore, MailerLite won't send emails directly from Gmail, Yahoo, or other email clients. This is because these email clients interfere with the deliverability of your mails. Instead, MailerLite wants an email address from a custom web domain to be your point of contact. Therefore, it is easiest to set up a custom domain and email and use these to complete your profile.

2.3.1. Website and custom email address

Firstly, what domain name are you going to use? Maybe it's YourName.com or YourNameWrites.com. Choose your domain name and purchase it. But this is just a name. MailerLite will not accept a domain name with just a holding page. They want to see an actual website, to know that you're a real person.

So, you will need to get a website to go with your new domain name. To this end, you need a web-hosting service and some website building tools. Building a website is beyond the scope of this book but there are other resources out there that can help you.

My strategy for this was to make the simplest website I could get away with and pass MailerLite's requirements. I had no intention of having a website myself until I realized it was a requirement for my newsletter platform, so it's still a single page with my branding, a list of my books, and a sign-up form for my newsletter. But this was enough for MailerLite to accept that it was a real operational website.

2.4. Navigating the MailerLite interface

When you log in to MailerLite, you will start on the **Dashboard**. This is an overview of the need-to-know-at-a-glance information about your account activity. Across the green bar at the top of the screen are several other tabs you can navigate to. **Campaigns** are emails you send individually – as opposed to a sequence of emails that send automatically when the sequence is triggered, as with the **Automation** tab.

Subscribers list the people who have signed up to receive your newsletter, as well as profile information about them (depending on what information they provided at sign-up), and any other tags (identifying information, e.g. "signed up via a Facebook campaign") that you assign to them.

Sites list the landing pages you create to point your sign-up links to. Basically, each landing page is a webpage where new members can enter whatever information you ask from them. By contrast, **Forms** are sign-up areas you put on your own webpage, either embedded into the page or as a pop-up on the website.

2.5. Branding and imagery

How do you represent yourself online?

To create a coherent and cohesive message, especially when you're starting out, it helps to have consistent branding on your social media, newsletter, and other online activities. At its simplest, this is an image that represents you, and can be your Facebook banner as well as the heading on your newsletter.

But what is that image? Is it the book you're currently promoting? Or the series it belongs to? What if you write another series?

I suggest you create your persona based on *you*, not any particular book. This will give you scope to go beyond one story, one series, or even one genre. If you're just starting, you may not know what way your future will unfold, so best to leave it open.

What image sums you up as a writer? I know of an author who wears red glasses and uses this as her brand because it is such a recognizable feature. If you are mostly in one genre, you could have a genre-invoking image e.g. planets and/or spaceship for science fiction, couple holding hands for sweet romance, magnifying glass for an amateur sleuth/cozy mystery, etc. My own image is a combination of my genre (fantasy) and my name (Everest) – a fantasy castle rising out of the clouds at the peak of Mt. Everest.

If you write with the same name in multiple genres, there may not be a single image that works for you. Perhaps you would prefer a composite image of all your 'genre images'. Maybe just your name in a font/color/placement that appeals to you. Whatever you pick, make sure you have the rights to use that image for that purpose (e.g. don't use a Facebook avatar, because you don't have a license to use that on other media).

There are plenty of reputable sites for stock photos, which allow you to buy the non-exclusive rights to an image for relatively little. **Shutterstock** is one of the best known, but **Deposit Photos** also has an excellent range. And if you keep an eye out, you will often find a sale on Deposit Photos for 100 image credits for $100 (and sometimes less!) A dollar an image is a very affordable way to both create your author branding and to find beautiful images to bring your newsletter stories to life.

I made this one using an image from Deposit Photos I got for $1, and a quick edit in Microsoft PowerPoint (it's what I have – there are other programs for free like Canva and BookBrush which do a great job for image manipulation, or Adobe Photoshop if you have more skills and are willing to invest in the software).

The reason I'm advising you to consider this branding upfront is that, once you have your image, you'll be using it on all sorts of content – starting with your email template, in the next section.

3. Creating an email template

Chapter Objectives

- *Designing a template that can be re-used for all your emails.*
- *Understanding the different elements of a newsletter email.*
- *Navigating the options for each element available in MailerLite.*
- *Building your email template.*

To start designing emails, click "Create Campaign" – either on the Campaign tab or from the Dashboard. You will need to enter a subject line for the email. The sender address and name will be pre-populated based on your account criteria in the "Who is it from?" section, but just check they are correct! If you have multiple pen names attached to the same account, you may need to change the sender name to match the readers you are contacting.

We will start by building a template so that the basics are in place and easy for you to reuse for future emails – set up your branding images, fonts, colors, and layouts. To this end, just name this first 'campaign' (i.e. email) some variant of "Template set up."

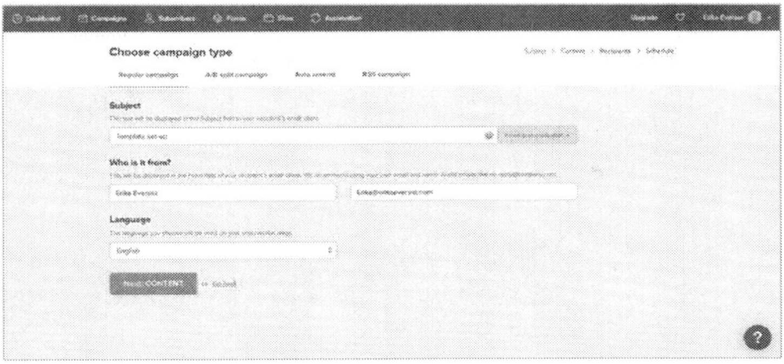

Once you save the set-up details, click forward to Content. You will get a choice of content editors. Personally, I use the Drag & Drop Editor, as it gives plenty of customization options without needing to be a computer coding guru!

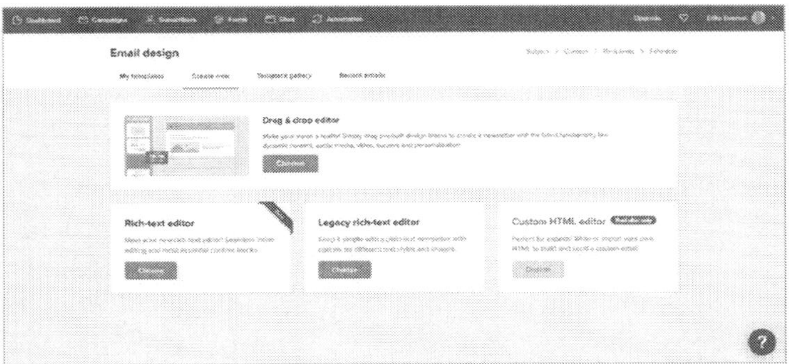

Next, you will need to select **Create New** (as you don't have any templates yet to choose from) and you will be brought to the email editor. I found this overwhelming at first. There are SO MANY options! And there is an example of an email layout in front of you…

I made the mistake initially of trying to take what MailerLite offered as an example, and change the pictures and text to match my message. It didn't suit me. After a bit of exploring through the column on the left-hand side, I discovered options that I liked much better. If you want to start with a fresh slate, so that you only include the building blocks *you* want, I suggest clicking on **Actions** tab in the black bar across the top of the page, and selecting the option "Remove content blocks."

Back to the column on the left. You can scroll through all the block options (there are a lot!) or use the drop-down filter at the top of the column to select a subset of related blocks to look at together e.g. Header, Footer, Content, Galleries, and more.

3.1. Email header

There are a lot of options within the **Header** blocks, depending on how you want to lay it out. Logo, navigation (with links to your website or other external pages), social media links (Facebook, Twitter, etc.).

Go back
Header
Logo
Logo + title
Logo + Navigation
Logo + horizontal navigation
Navigation
Logo + social links

But here is a tip I worked out the hard way: *just because it's not in the list of header blocks, doesn't mean you can't use it as your header.*

What this meant for me is that I chose to use a picture as a banner/header instead of a logo or links. This is why I suggested in the previous section that you consider an image to encapsulate your writing. Note that MailerLite has a limit of 2MB for images, so make sure any picture you create is under this limit. To add a picture as your banner, first, drag an **Image** block from the block list (in the Content sub-list) to the top of your email.

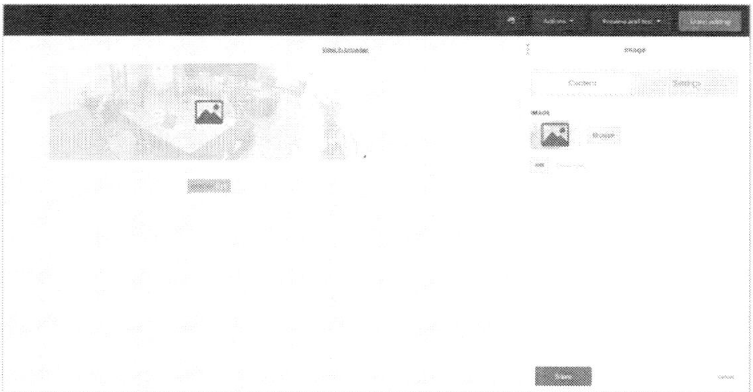

Click **Browse** to access your MailerLite image library. To upload an image (in this case, the author banner just created) click the orange "Upload image" button in the top right corner. You can upload from your computer, or from external sources such as Google Drive.

Previously uploaded images will be displayed in your library under this search bar. Once you have the desired image, click the "select" option for that image to import it into the image block in your email to create your banner.

Personally, I prefer the look of a banner that spans the whole page, so I chose the "Edge to Edge" image width, but you can play around with the options on the Settings tab until you find what works for you.

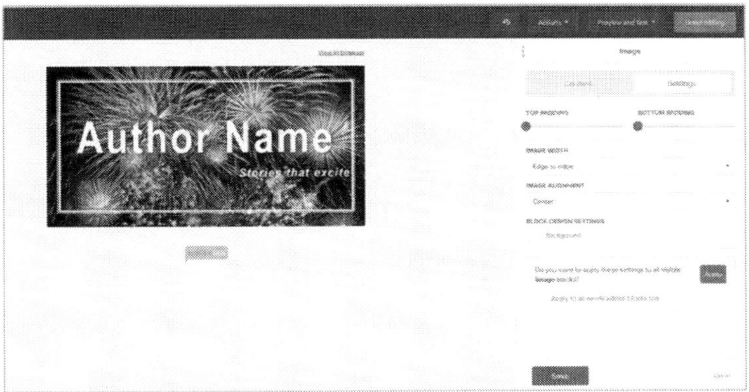

In the URL box on the Content tab, you can add a link to the image so that clicking on it will take the reader to the link specified. For example, you could have it linking to your website or your Facebook page. I don't bother with this for two reasons. Firstly, as I have said before, my website is still sparse and not ready for receiving traffic yet (it's on my to-do list!) Secondly, this is the top of my newsletter; I don't want to direct people away from it just yet! I want them to read it, so I won't place a link to pull them away before they have a chance to read the content.

Top and bottom padding control the blank space above and below the block. I use none for the banner image, but padding for other blocks may be more useful e.g. between blocks of text. The padding is controlled through the Settings panel for all blocks.

3.2. Email footer

MailerLite offers four design options for the footer of your email. You can experiment with the different options to see which layout suits you best, but the essential components of the email footer are:

- Your sender name and physical address, as we spoke about with regards to the CAN-SPAM Act,
- Your social media links, if you haven't already included them in the header, and
- Your unsubscribe message and link.

3.2.1. Company details

MailerLite will automatically populate your company address from the details you filled out at registration, but you can modify these by going to the edit panel on the right-hand side and filling in new details. As you can see here, I have redacted my company address for these screenshots. You can also include a phone number, email address, or any other forms of contact you want to make available.

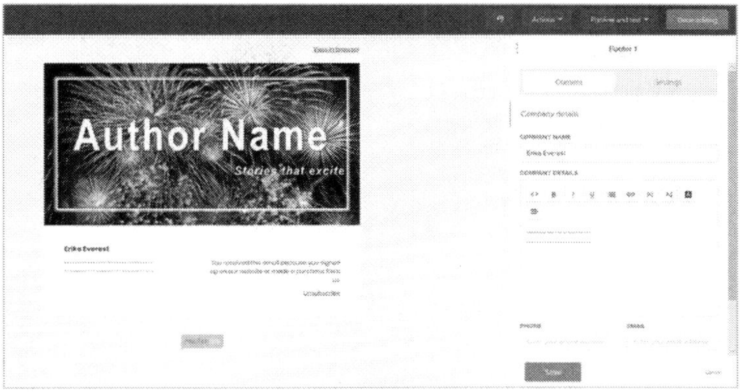

3.2.2. Social links

You don't see the social media links initially, as in the picture above. When you open the editing panel it gives you an option of certain standard social media sites that you can add. Once you add the address of that account, the icon for that social media site will appear in your footer, and when readers click on that icon it will bring them to the link that you entered.

Facebook, Twitter, Instagram… there are many social media platforms, and you may or may not have them, but I would encourage you to consider some author-specific ones that might be of use. For example, BookBub, GoodReads, your Amazon profile page. So, pick the ones that you use and are appropriate to your business (you can add more later as you expand your social media presence), add your links, and those icons will appear on the screen.

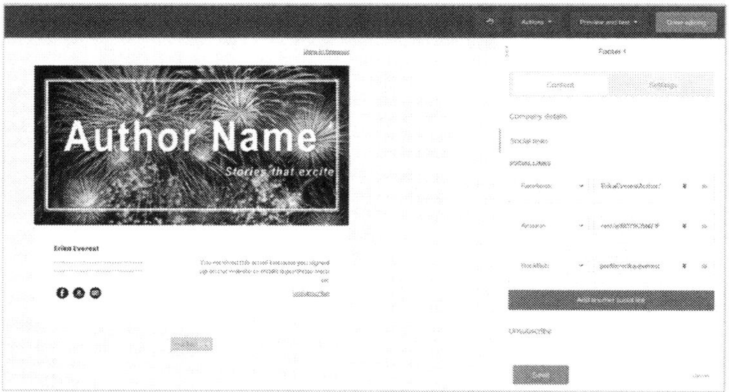

Going to the Settings tab allows you further customization options for your social links' appearance: shape, size, and color. The previous image shows **Shape** = Circle and **Color** = Black. You can see the difference changing these to Default and Color respectively make in the image below.

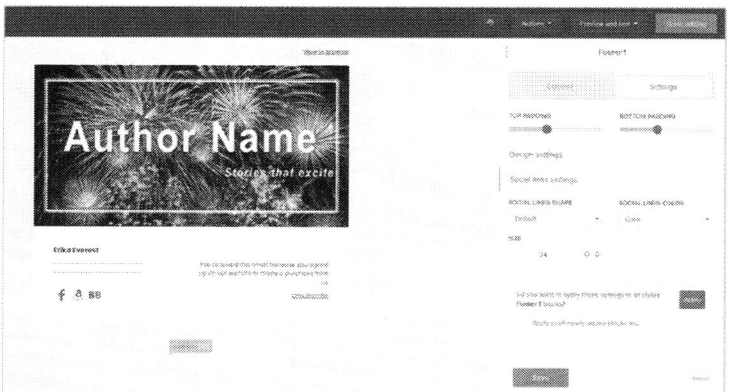

3.2.3. Unsubscribe

Finally, you must have an unsubscribe message. There are two parts to this: the **disclaimer**, which tells the reader why you sent them this newsletter, and the **unsubscribe button** itself, which is just a piece of text with a link to take them off the mailing list. You can customize that piece of text as the default simply reads, "unsubscribe." You can make it say something else, like "Goodbye, I'm gone" or "It's not me, it's you," but by-and-large "unsubscribe" does the job and keeps it unobtrusive. You don't want to keep members on your mailing list who aren't your readers and are ultimately costing you, either in terms of paying for your subscriber numbers or in your deliverability and engagement rates. But at the same time, you don't want to make it too easy for new joiners to exit. You want them to try and read your newsletter for a while to get used to your style and maybe find the value in it that makes them want to stick around, giving you a chance to convert them to a true fan.

The disclaimer text is an awkward one. The default simply says "you received this email because you signed up on our website or made a purchase from us." That's not really true for most author newsletters, so we need something else. Because of the way the onboarding sequence is set up, you likely gave away a reader magnet, a book, as an incentive for receiving your newsletter. Maybe they signed up on your website or Facebook page and subsequently received the magnet. Perhaps they got the magnet originally from a BookFunnel or StoryOrigin promotion and were added to your list as a consequence. Either way, when they start on your list, they get that book. Thus, to make people understand why they're getting your email, you can say something like "you signed up to my mailing list when you downloaded your copy of <reader

magnet title>." This will be true no matter which entry point they've come from, and it reminds the recipient why they are getting this email that they may have forgotten about. This especially helps to avoid people marking your email as unsolicited or spam, if they choose to unsubscribe.

You may wish to put some additional text in the disclaimer, e.g. "you can unsubscribe from my newsletter at any time, but I hope you won't" or some other more personalized request to retain those who are a good fit for staying.

Whatever text you decide on goes in your disclaimer box, and then your email footer will look like this:

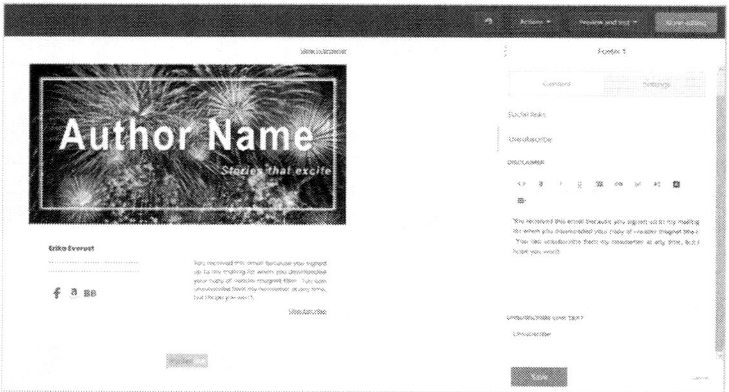

3.3. Email body

Now we have the header and footer in place, it's time to build a template for the content.

3.3.1. Text

The piece of content you will use most frequently is the **Text** block There is also a block called a **Text Box** but this is more suited to a quote or piece of text that you want to highlight, and not as part of your general message. The default text block has some Lorem Ipsum filler and is center aligned.

There are plenty of text formatting options that can be applied to the text block. Within the Content tab, from left to right, the controls are:

- HTML
- Bold
- Italic
- Underline
- List (i.e. Bullet points)
- Link
- Variable
- Size
- Text color
- Align

For illustration, I'll choose justified alignment in the following example, but I'll change the color, size, and font in the Settings tab, rather than via the text options in the Content tab. This is because the Settings control the default appearance of the entire block, whereas the Content controls are only local overrides, used, for example, to highlight a particular phrase in the message you are writing in that block.

I've chosen size 14 Verdana in blue, which can be selected from the Settings panel as shown in the next image. Note the hexadecimal code for your color (in this case, #007bff) so that you can apply it to text in other blocks to maintain consistency throughout your email.

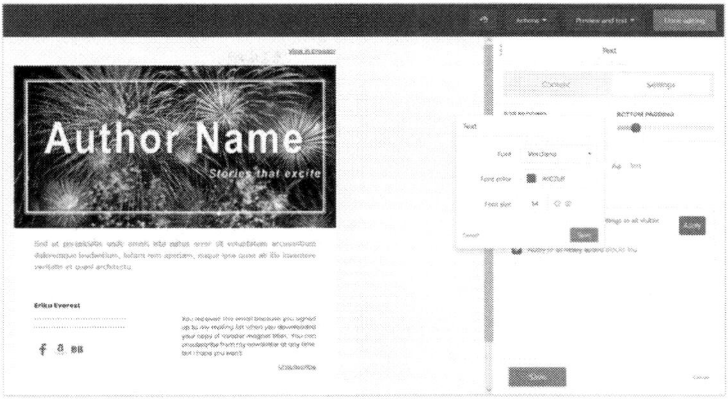

Take some time playing around with fonts, font size, font color, and alignment, to find your ideal presentation. Now when you want to create text in an email, you can copy this text block and use it again and again.

3.3.2. Graphics

How important are pictures to your aesthetic?

Personally, I love them. I like how they break up a long page of text. But I also recognize that the more pictures you include, the larger the total file size of your email will be, which could affect deliverability to some email providers.

If you think you will use images – or even *might* use images – in some of your newsletters, then I suggest that you would set them up as part of your template, so that it is an easy matter to include a picture if you chose to, without needing to spend a lot of effort ensuring the appearance of the picture is consistent with the rest of your email at the time you want to send it.

In the blocks list, the subset **Gallery** provides different configurations of pictures, grouping two, three, four and more pictures together. But these are just images, similar to a collage. If you want to include text with your image, either to explain it or because you want to have an image as only part of your newsletter with text running alongside it, then you need to select some of the "image + text" blocks from the Content sub-list.

If you add these to the template now, apply the same font settings as you did for your main text block to maintain consistency. You will also see that these blocks have some other options for text, such as heading and subheading. You can choose to omit these headers from your email by leaving the fields blank, but if you wish to include them you can also specify their color and appearance through the settings tab. The picture itself can either be medium, i.e. half the width of your page, or small, which is one-third of the width of your page, depending on the balance of text to picture you desire.

Select the blocks that you think will appeal most to your readers. Spend the time adjusting the settings so that the text is consistent with your text blocks and they are appropriately laid out. I would suggest, even if you don't think you'll use them, to update the presentation of the header and sub-header areas. It is easy to delete that text when you use the block, at which point the formatting doesn't matter, but if you don't format it now and decide later you want it, then it is more time consuming to have to set that up on a case by case basis each time you use it.

I have left the default image in place along with the default text so that I know what my template looks like and it is easy to change the content later. Here is my template: my picture header, my text block, my text and image blocks, and my footer, ready for use.

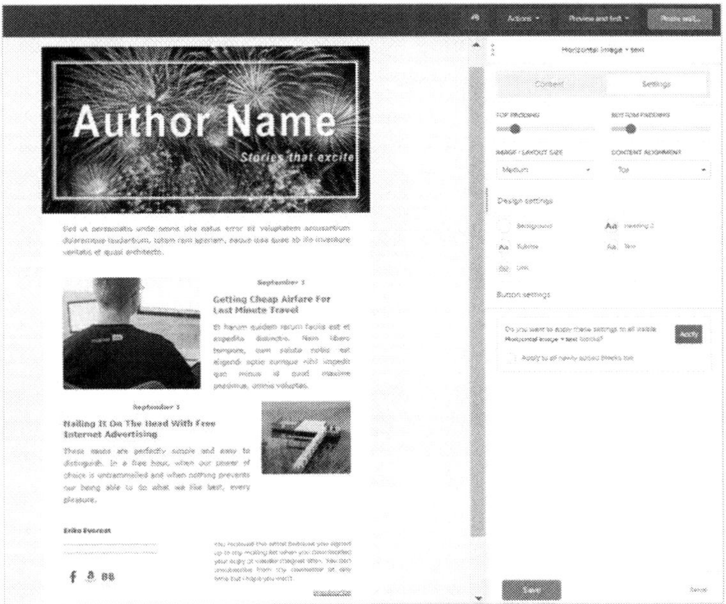

3.3.3. Links

We have discussed creating links out of pictures in the header section and creating social media links in the footer section, but if you want to include links in the main body of your email – and I assume you do, as how else will we sell books? – then there are two ways to do this. The first is an inline link. This is where the text says "click here to read more" and the "here" is highlighted as a link to click. You might use this if you are directing people to a blog or perhaps to a review you wrote on BookBub. This can be achieved using the text options above. When you select the **Link** icon, it lets you specify what link to direct to and what text should appear on the screen. These can be the same, e.g. when you want to direct someone to your website or blog. Alternatively, you may prefer just to say "here," as above, and not include the long identifier string if it is not an easy address to remember. The appearance of inline links is governed by the link option in the Settings Tab so make sure these are set up to reflect how you wish the links to appear (e.g. underlined, a different font color, etc.).

The second option is to create a Button, whose sole purpose is to be clicked. In the **Buttons** sub-list of the Blocks inventory, there are many button blocks to choose from. The most commonly used, for us as authors, is the single-button block. But if for some reason you need two, three, or four buttons, those blocks are also available. A button can be set up with the directional link behind it and different text on the button, similar to the inline link. A button draws attention to this link in a way the inline link doesn't. For example, to download a copy of your reader magnet, the text on a button can say "get my book" or something similar, and the URL behind it can point to the BookFunnel download page (which we'll talk about later). You can also use this button to direct people to a sales page, perhaps using a universal book link like books2read or geni.us, so they have just one click from your page to their preferred sales platform. The URL and button text can be customized on the **Contents** tab.

If you are involved in a promotion and you wish to direct people to that promotional page, you can use a button to say "take me to free books." Another option here, of course, is a picture link. Many promotions come with a graphic and you can insert this graphic as a picture into your newsletter and make it your link as well, so that whether people click the picture or the button they will be taken where they need to go.

Finally, you can control the look of your button through the **Settings** tab. Make it big, make it obvious – you want people to click. But also try to make the colors in line with the color palette in the rest of your newsletter. For our sample newsletter here, I'm going to use the same pink as in the headers as I feel this is a nice counterpoint to the blue text and picks up colors in the author header banner too. So here is my button:

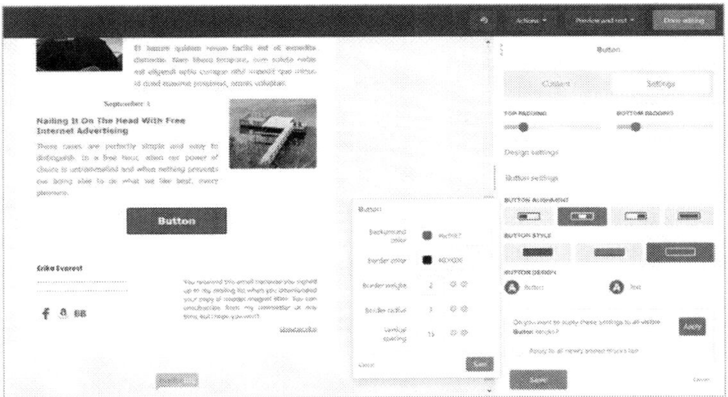

3.3.4. Section breaks

Back at the top level, on the right-hand panel, there are three options for controlling the overall look of your template: List, Card, and Full width. **List** is the view we have been using up to now, which stacks each block one after another. **Full width** is the same as List except that the white space expands the entire width of the screen. Personally, I find this looks a little odd because the text of your newsletter is still in the same column it has always been; there is just not the gray background around your newsletter anymore.

Card separates the blocks, putting space between them, creating natural delineation between the sections in your newsletter.

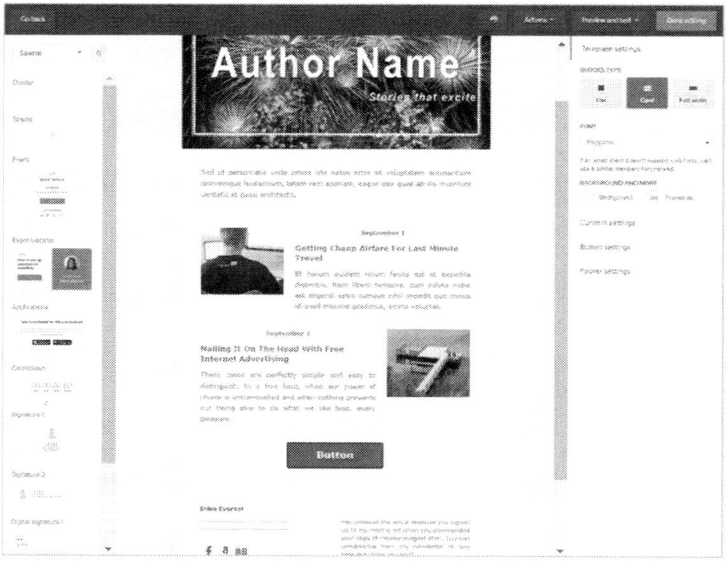

This works if you want to differentiate your sections *and* if every block is a separate section. It does *not* work if you want to have multiple blocks in the same section, as it's an all-or-nothing option. For example, if you want to have a text block, then a text + horizontal image, followed by another text block (so that the text appears to wrap-around the picture), that will be three separate blocks and the Card option would have gaps between each of them, even though the text content may flow continuously through each of those blocks.

A way to create delineation in your newsletter without relying on Card – thereby allowing you to have multiple blocks in each section – is to use a special divider to mark your section breaks. You can find this in the **Special** block sub-list (visible in the previous picture). The section break can either be a line (**Divider**) or a deliberate piece of blank space (**Spacer**).

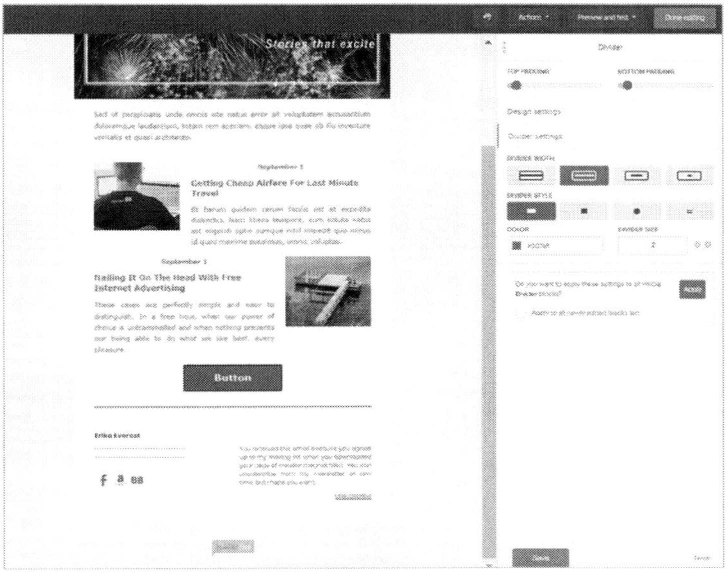

If you're including section breaks, you may also want to include headings for your different sections. You can get these as **Titles** from the Contents block sub-list. Again, multiple options are available for Titles, so pick the one that suits you best and make sure to format your text and appearance to match your color schemes.

If you know upfront that you want to have specific sections in every email, and that they will form part of your standard layout, then you may want to create those headings and breaks here in your template, to save you from having to type them each time. If you are not sure about this, check out the chapter "What should I say?" to decide if this approach is right for you. If you don't plan to have titles in every section, or if the titles may change from mail to mail, then you don't need to create multiple headers in your template. A single sample header is sufficient, and you can copy and change this as many times as you need when creating your individual emails.

3.3.5. Personalization and custom fields

The **Variable** option within the text panel inserts the value of that variable for the specific subscriber you are writing to. The one variable you will always have populated is the email address, because a reader can't sign up to a newsletter without one. You could use this, for example, in your Unsubscribe message, saying something like "this email was sent to [email address] because you bought my book. If you no longer wish to receive emails from me…" All other fields are optional to collect, though I would always advise getting a name, at least. If you have a name, you can use this to personalize the email.

Instead of a generic "Hello from the writing cave," you can start with "Hello [name]" and MailerLite will insert the appropriate name for the subscriber you are writing to ("Hello Mike," "Hello Grace," etc.).

Instead of – or possibly in addition to – putting this in the body of the email, you can also include a name in your subject line. Research has shown that emails that are personalized in the subject line are more likely to be opened. However, fatigue can set in if this is overused. If every email starts with the subscriber's name, e.g. "Jim, great deal for you," "Jim, new release update," it loses its effectiveness.

If you're using a variable, you must make sure that if that subscriber's value is blank the variable still makes sense. For example, "Hello ," (if no name is provided) looks a bit odd and a bit unprofessional. So, if you are using a field that is not mandatory for subscribers to provide a value for, you need to think about whether it is appropriate to include this field in your personalization. One way around this is to put an alternate text to use if the personalization is not available. You can specify this by putting a pipe symbol (vertical bar; |) and the alternate text to the side. For example, in a salutation, you could say "Hello sleuth" (e.g. for a cozy mystery readership) and you'd specify this as "Hello [name] | sleuth." If the name field is populated (e.g. with Mike), the salutation would be filled in as "Hello Mike" but if someone has given you their email address but not their name the salutation will appear as "Hello sleuth."

There are many other fields you can collect and you need to decide which ones are right for you. By default, MailerLite includes Email, Name, Last Name, Company, Country, City, Phone, State, and ZIP.

You can also specify **custom fields** that aren't on the drop-down list, by specifying what you want to call that variable yourself. You can see from the image above that I added a variable called “device.” This allows me to target people who read on Kindle, an iPhone or Android app, or on a Nook, Kobo, or other devices. I can use this to say in the subject line “Calling all [device] users” which will appear as “Calling all Kobo users” or “Calling all Kindle users” etc. It is personalization in a different way because it speaks to the subscriber without using their name. But if there is a blank for this field, “Calling all users” doesn't make sense. “Calling all insert platform here users” is not so great either! So, if you include a personalized variable in the subject line, you do need to consider how well the personalization will fit the overall context and whether it would look odd if that personalization is missing.

3.4. Preview mode

In the black ribbon across the top of your screen, there is a button marked **Preview and test**. If you click this, two options appear in the drop-down list. The first is **Preview mode** and the second is **Send a test email**.

Clicking Preview mode will show you what your email will look like to your recipients in both the desktop version and mobile version. Assuming you've been building your newsletter on your computer, the desktop version will look very much like what you've already worked on. Therefore, you'll mainly need to check the mobile version, in case some things appear differently from the way you want them to. These days most people will view on a cellphone or tablet, so it's important that your email is optimized for mobile use. Some things to look out for are that the order of pictures relative to your text may be switched from what you expected, and if you use justified alignment some lines may have odd spacing as there are fewer words possible in the width of a mobile screen compared to a desktop screen. Also, the overall length of your email may appear differently, and you may want to think about how many times the reader has to scroll up on a phone to get your full message (and if that's desirable or not).

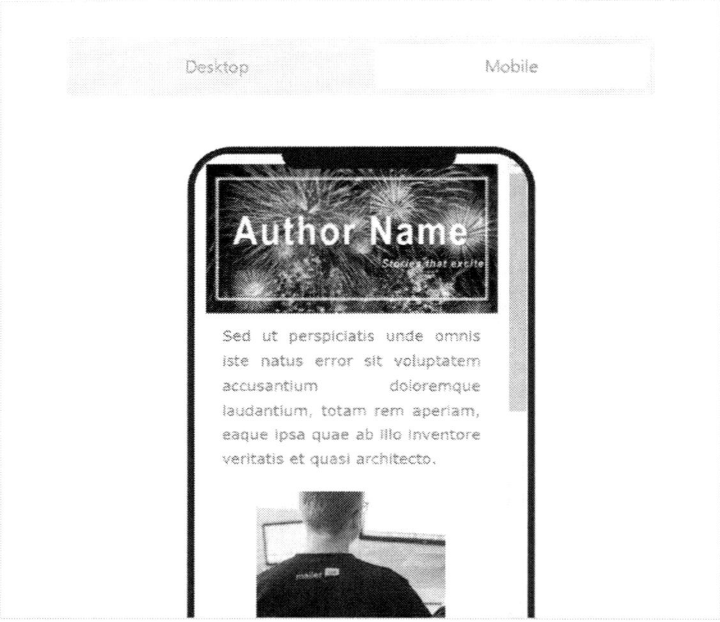

Many of these considerations can only truly be checked when you have live content to review as the template won't show the exact message you are sending. After reviewing the previews of both desktop and mobile, you can return to your template and make edits to the layout, and repeat the process as many times as necessary.

Once the preview cycle is complete and you're satisfied with your output, send yourself a test email. This allows you to see the newsletter in practice. It's similar to a preview but also gives you the chance to see other details, like how the subject line will appear in your inbox. You may also want to send a test email to a friend, to look it over and check that you haven't missed something obvious, without having to wait for the full campaign to be sent.

With these steps complete, your template is as ready as it can be. Click on the **Actions** button in the black ribbon and select **Save as template**.

This will prompt you to enter a name for the email you have just created. I suggest simply "Template," or some variation thereof.

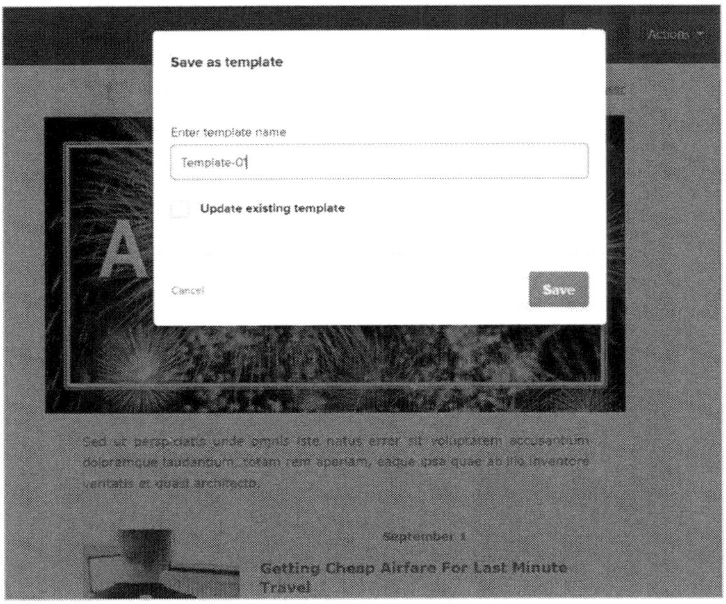

When you have saved your template, click the green **Done editing** button in the top right-hand corner. This will prompt you to select recipients for your email, as MailerLite assumes that this is a real campaign you want to send, and not just you creating your template. Ignore what comes up on the next screen. Instead, toggle back to dashboard or some other part of MailerLite. Your template is saved in the Campaigns tab under drafts. We will look at how to recall the template and use it when we start building workflows and campaigns in a later chapter.

4. Elements of a workflow (automation sequence)

Chapter Objectives

- *Exploring the five elements available for building a workflow – Trigger, Email, Delay, Condition, and Action – and the purpose of each.*
- *Understanding the options available within each element.*
- *Learning about dividing your mailing list using 'tags' to identify shared traits of subscribers.*

4.1. Trigger

There are six triggers that can initiate an automated sequence, or workflow.

- **When subscriber joins a group**: this is when you tag them to become a member of a particular group when they sign up to your mailing list and is the one you will use most often. The next section describes what tagging means and how to do it.
- **When subscriber completes a form**: forms are how people sign up to your newsletter. While this could be the direct trigger, instead I assign the subscriber to a group when they complete a form, and then use 'joins a group' as the onboarding trigger. I prefer this

because the group assignment is a permanent tag that provides information about the subscriber.

- **When a subscriber clicks a link**: this can be useful if there is a second automated sequence that you think only a subset of your list will be interested in. E.g. *This mailing list is for my science fiction series, but a few years ago I also wrote a 4-book cozy mystery series. If you would like to learn more about it, click here.* Clicking that link then triggers a new sequence, introducing your cozy series.
- **Updated field**: as the name suggests, this triggers a workflow when some details on your subscriber's profile have been updated. Mostly, subscribers will only get to enter profile details when they initially sign up, so this trigger has limited use for us. But if you allow subscribers to add new information to their profile (which will be discussed in Section 8.4) then this trigger could be used to email them to confirm receipt of their updated data.
- **The anniversary of a date**: birthdays are the most obvious use for this trigger (assuming your subscribers have elected to give you that information), but another option is the anniversary of joining your list. E.g. Thank you for being with me for another year; your support means the world to me.
- **The exact match of a date**: if you want to start a workflow with a few emails around a launch or promotion date, this is the trigger to use, tied to a once-off specific date.

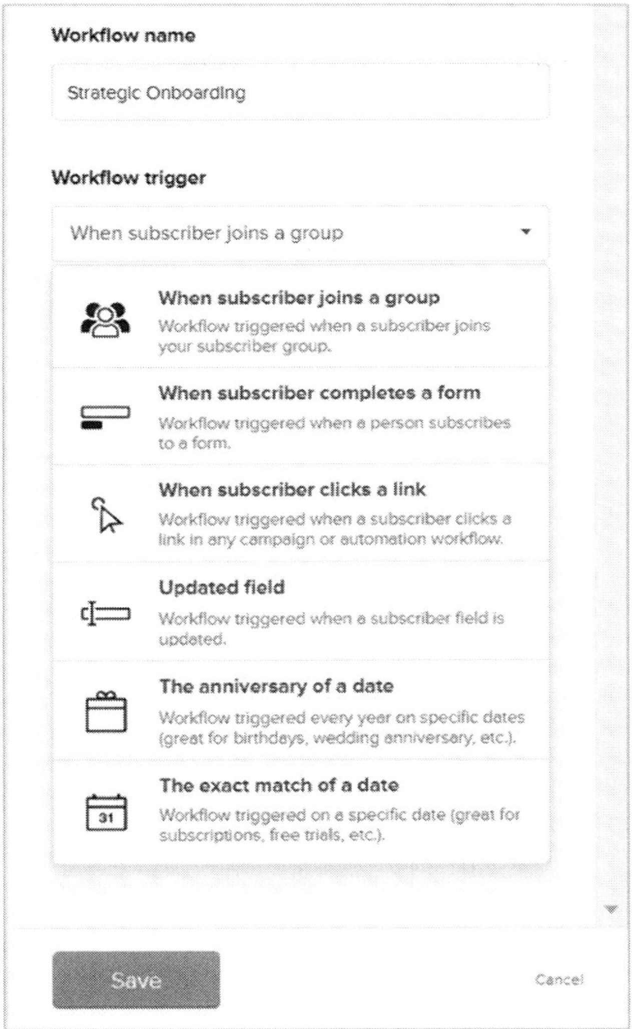
Workflow name
Strategic Onboarding
Workflow trigger
When subscriber joins a group
When subscriber joins a group
Workflow triggered when a subscriber joins your subscriber group.
When subscriber completes a form
Workflow triggered when a person subscribes to a form.
When subscriber clicks a link
Workflow triggered when a subscriber clicks a link in any campaign or automation workflow.
Updated field
Workflow triggered when a subscriber field is updated.
The anniversary of a date
Workflow triggered every year on specific dates (great for birthdays, wedding anniversary, etc.).
The exact match of a date
Workflow triggered on a specific date (great for subscriptions, free trials, etc.).
Save
Cancel

4.1.1. Tagging and group membership

Assigning subscribers to groups, or tagging them, is a means of identifying traits relevant to particular subscribers. There are two broad categories of traits I like to track. The first is about where they've come from and other origin traits. The second relates to decisions I want to make in the future about the subscribers, to help me parse them as to what actions I need to take when sending them newsletters.

Origin traits include how and from where they signed up for your newsletter. Was it through your Amazon author page, a Facebook ad, a promotion you ran, back matter from one of your books, something another author shared in *their* newsletter? Knowing the source of your subscribers can help you in two ways:

1. You know what's most successful and can do more of it and
2. You may want to treat them differently, depending on where they come from.

In particular, sign-ups who come from the back matter of one of your books (i.e. after "the end" where you say "if you want to learn more sign up to my newsletter") are known as **organic subscribers**.

Organic is a word that is used a lot, and it can mean different things in different contexts. It has a different meaning in terms of advertising and sales than it does for newsletter subscribers. The simplest definition is that an organic subscriber is one who has read your book and *then* signed up for your newsletter, as opposed to someone who signs up in order to get a book from you. (Even if they love your book and stay on your mailing list, they didn't *know* they would love it when they signed up). By contrast, an organic subscriber has just read something by you and has asked for more. Those subscribers are at a different level of appreciation and are already well on their way to becoming super fans. So how you interact with them is going to be a little different from the subscribers you need to 'warm-up' first.

Decision traits tell you what types of emails these people need to get. Organic or not is one such trait as it can influence future actions. Other things that may matter are whether or not they need to get your cookie/reader magnet (which will talk about in the next chapter). Certain promotions give the magnet out immediately and collect email addresses for you to import to your mailing list in batches later, in which case you would not want to send those subscribers the reader magnet again when you add them to your list. If you sell your reader magnet as well as give it away for newsletter subscribers, you wouldn't want to send your reader magnet to someone who had already bought it and *then* signed up to your newsletter either! Such a person would actually be an *organic* subscriber because they signed up after reading something by you.

Another useful tag is the **Onboarding** tag. This basically says "I want this subscriber to go through my onboarding sequence." You may have several onboarding sequences for different series or the like, so you might want to specify a different pattern of emails for each of them and that's fine, but by-and-large I would expect that all subscribers will be going through the same onboarding sequence. You might think "well, if everyone does it why do I need to make a group to specify it?" The answer is above: you need a trigger to start a workflow, and this is as good as any. By assigning them to the onboarding group, you immediately insert them into a workflow that will deliver your emails to them.

The final tag that is useful is **Regular**, i.e. the group to whom you will send your regular monthly, bi-weekly, or whatever frequency, mailings. This is so the people in your warm-up/onboarding sequence don't get your regular emails before they have fully warmed up, and so you have a way of distinguishing people depending on their stage.

With the exception of REGULAR, all of these tags are assigned when your subscriber initially signs up. How these tags are attached to each subscriber is covered in Chapter 8, *Signing up*. REGULAR is assigned once the subscriber has completed the onboarding sequence. As such, how to assign it is covered in Chapter 7, *Building the onboarding sequence.*

In summary, the tags that I suggest you set up are

- **Onboarding**, for everybody who's going through that welcome sequence
- **Deliver-Cookie**, for the people you want to receive the cookie (don't assign this tag to anyone who's received the cookie already or shouldn't receive it for some other reason)
- **Organic**, for people who click a link at the back of one of your books (any other link is non-organic, and does not get the tag)
- The sign-up sources that you can consider are as many as places you can think to put your sign-up link. You can create a different link for every location (and we'll talk more about this in the chapter on sign-ups). But for now, some options to consider are
    - **Signup-Source-Amazon**, for Amazon author page
    - **Signup-Source-Facebook**, for a Facebook Post
    - **Signup-Source-Facebook-Ad1**, for a Facebook ad (and you might want a different link for each ad to really know which ones are working)

  - **Signup-Source-BookFunnel**, for a BookFunnel promotion (and similar for other promotion sites)
  - **Signup-Source-Book1**, **Signup-Source-Book2**, etc., for the back matter of your own books
  - **Signup-Source-Jane's-Feb-Newsletter**, for a shout out in another author's newsletter
  - Etc.
- **Regular**, for the people who have completed your onboarding sequence and receive your regular campaigns.

You may find you want additional tags later related to special steps of your workflow. We will discuss that during the workflow build in Chapter 7.

4.2. Email

When you add an email to a workflow, you will be asked for a **Subject** for the email (which can include emojis and/or personalization, e.g. the subscriber's name). The name and email address you are sending from appear in the **Who is it from?** section. This is pre-populated with the details that you used when you set up the account, which can be edited.

In the Email Content section, there is a button to "Design email" – this will bring you away from the workflow to a separate page where you create the content of your email (e.g. text, pictures, links, etc. as described in Chapter 3.)

There is a check-box to select **Google Analytics** for your email. This tracks clicks from your email to your website, provided you have Google Analytics set up on your website. Personally, I don't see this as a huge advantage to authors. We are more likely to be directing subscribers to Amazon or some other sales platform. Even if you do direct sales, it may be through a site like Shopify, so tracking clicks to your website may not be the greatest value. On the other hand, it doesn't hurt and it costs nothing, so I usually turn it on for my emails anyway.

Finally, there is a **Language** selection. I'm assuming if you are reading this, you will probably select English, but there are a *lot* of other options available. This is not the language of your newsletter content, but the language in which your unsubscribe instructions will be written (every email requires these instructions, as discussed in Section 3.2.3.) Pick the language that is appropriate to the majority of your subscribers – which is whatever language you write in.

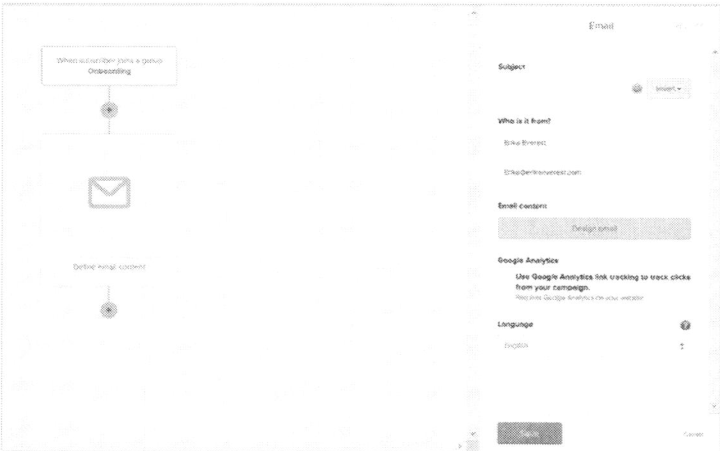

4.3. Delay

Delays can either be for a set number of units – minutes, days, weeks, or months – or until a particular time point is achieved.

Such time points include time of day, day of the week, day of the month, or even one date in the year. Each of the last three time points also allows you to schedule the time your next step in the workflow will occur, on the day chosen.

For the day of the month, if you chose 29th, 30th, or 31st, the months in which those dates don't occur will not have a workflow sent, but you can choose "last day of the month" instead if that's what you are aiming for.

If you want a particular day of the week/time of the month combination, e.g. the first Thursday of each month, you can achieve this by stacking delays. The first delay will be "wait until the last day of the month" and the second will be "wait until the day of the week is Thursday." (The reason for doing the last day of the previous month instead of the first day of the target month is that if the month starts on a Thursday, the second delay will wait until the following Thursday, i.e. the 8th, which would be the second Thursday of the month.)

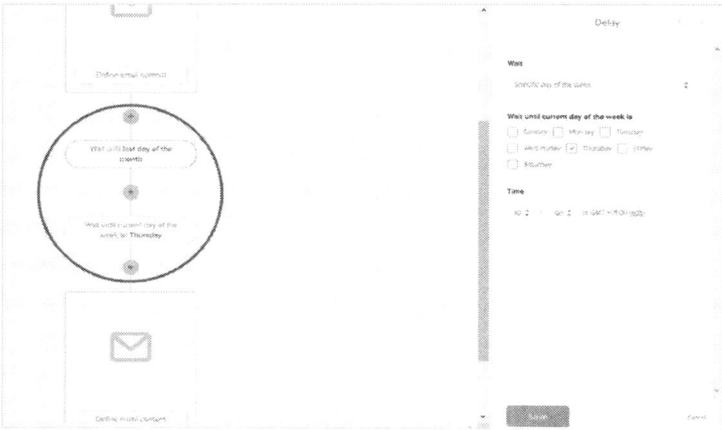

4.4. Condition

There are five conditions that can be used to filter subscribers through your workflow.

1. Campaign activity
2. Workflow activity
3. Custom fields
4. Group membership
5. Segment membership

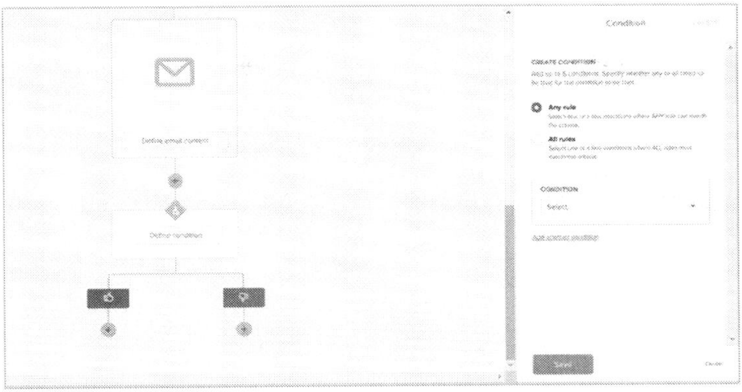

(4) and (5) are similar in that you simply select the group/segment that contains the specific subscribers you want.

(1) and (2) are likewise similar. Campaign refers to a regular email and workflow refers to an email in *the current* automation sequence. You will be asked to select which email you want to refer to, and then what activity in that email you want to define your condition on. The options are:

- Had any link clicked
- Had a specific link clicked
- Was opened and did not have a specific link clicked
- Was not opened
- Was opened
- Was opened with no links clicked

If you select one of the options referring to a specific link, you will get one further drop-down list with all the links in your email to choose from.

Custom fields are entries in your database about your subscribers (see Chapter 3). You collect name and email address at sign-up, but can also request other information such as birthday, country, etc. In (3) above, you can use custom fields to create a condition. For example, you wouldn't want to tell your Kobo readers about a series that is in Kindle Unlimited, and thus not available to them as it is exclusive to Amazon (you would need to collect a custom field based on preferred platform, for this).

Finally, you can have up to five conditions stacked. And you can choose if all of the conditions need to apply to the selection, or if any one of the conditions is acceptable.

E.g. you have a Kindle countdown deal coming up and you want to inform your US and UK readers, but not annoy your other readers who cannot take advantage of the offer. So, you want to create a condition that selects subscribers who are in the US or UK.

- ANY condition met
    - Condition 1: custom fields
        - location = US
    - Condition 2: custom fields
        - location = UK

Another example: you want to run a re-engagement campaign for people who signed up via a BookFunnel promo, but have opened *none* of the emails in your onboarding sequence

- ALL conditions met
    - Condition 1: Group Membership
        - Group = SignupSouce_BookFunnel
    - Condition 2: Workflow activity
        - Email = Welcome
            - Activity = Was not opened
    - Condition 3: Workflow activity
        - Email = Email #2

        - Activity = Was not opened
- Condition 4: Workflow activity
    - Email = Email #3
        - Activity = Was not opened

If you want a more complicated condition, where some elements require a positive response and others a negative (e.g. Facebook sign-up but *not* in the US) – and you can rephrase one of the elements so they are all positive or all negative, then you can stack conditions as separate steps in your workflow.

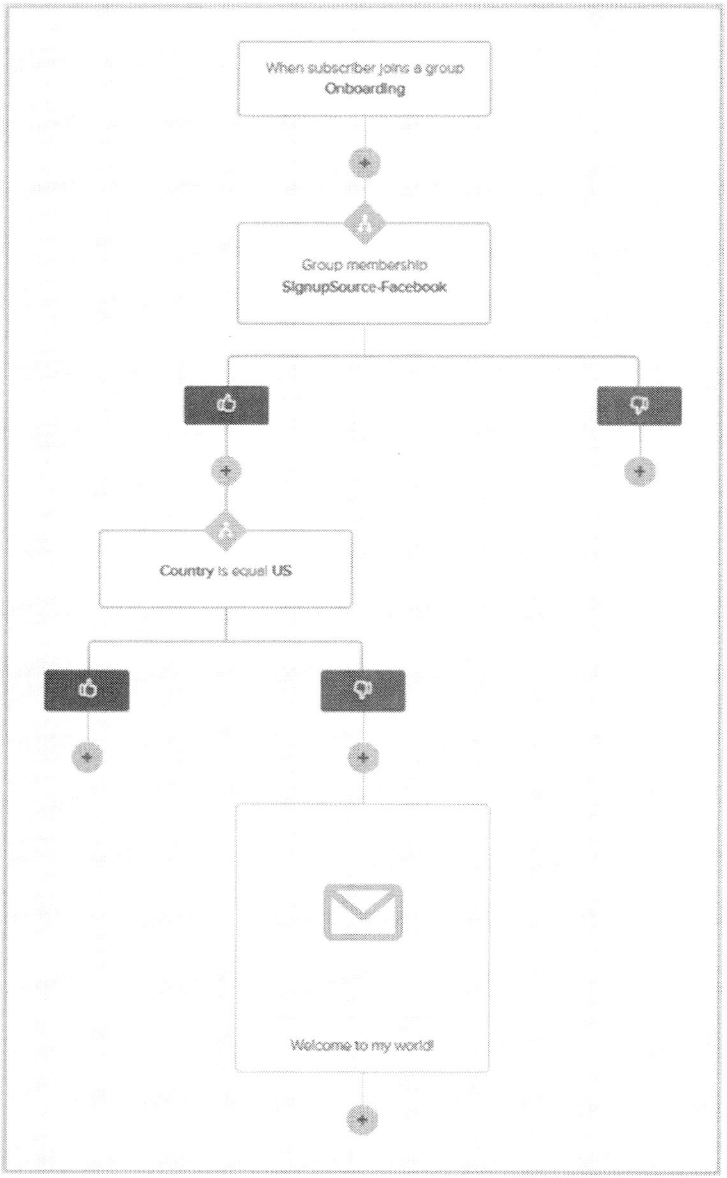
When subscriber joins a group
Onboarding
Group membership
SignupSource-Facebook
Country is equal US
Welcome to my world!

It is important to include Delays before Condition steps, to ensure there is time for the subscriber to meet the condition before the outcome is assessed.

4.5. Action

There are 6 actions that you can take at any point during your workflow:

1. Update custom field
2. Copy to group
3. Move to group
4. Remove from group
5. Mark as unsubscribed
6. Move to another step

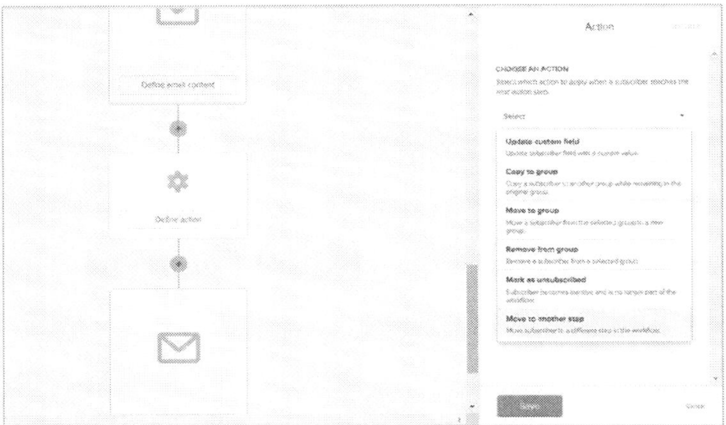

(2) adds a subscriber to a group and (4) removes a subscriber from a group, as the names suggest. In both cases, once you select the action you get a drop-down list of the groups to which you wish the action to apply. (3) is a combination of

these, in that it removes the subscriber from one group and adds them to another instead. Both groups need to be specified when this action is chosen.

(6) is the action I have found most useful. This allows you to start in one place, but then join into the main branch of the workflow somewhere else. For example, if you have sign-ups from two different sources – one from a promotion you did with several other authors and another from a Facebook post – you might want to acknowledge those sources in your onboarding sequence. In the first case, you might have a custom welcome email reminding them of the promotion they found you through, but after that initial welcome, you want them to get the same emails as the subscriber who signed up via Facebook. Moving to another step allows you to jump into the queue of the main sequence, so you have one welcome email that's different for each source followed by the same subsequent emails for everyone, so there is consistency in your message.

If you select action (5), mark as unsubscribed, the person will be removed from your active subscriber list and you will not be able to send them further emails. However, a subject removed from the active list in this way will not be sent the “thank you for unsubscribing” message, and thus will not be given the option to report your email as Spam.

Finally, if you choose the action to update a custom field (1), you will get a drop-down list to select which field you want to update and then which value you want to assign it. I don't use custom fields for non-personalized values (and the value assigned here is the same for all subscribers, and author-specified not subscriber-specified) because I use Groups to identify subscribers with the same trait (e.g. completed onboarding sequence). Because of this approach I take, I don't see the value of this particular option for newsletters. But you may see a use for it in your business.

5. Cookies and reader magnets

Chapter Objectives

- *Understanding the purpose of cookies and reader magnets, and the difference between them.*
- *Determining a good subject for a reader magnet.*
- *Using BookFunnel to distribute your reader magnet.*
- *Evaluating the pricing strategy for reading magnets.*

A **reader magnet** is something you offer to new readers to encourage them to try your work and get them to sign up to your mailing list at the same time. A **cookie** is a free gift or incentive you offer to someone who has already read your book to encourage them to sign up for your mailing list. These may sound the same, but a cookie has more options than a reader magnet.

For example, someone who has just read your book may be very interested to read a deleted scene, a bonus scene set three years in the future, or the back story for a character. Maybe a family tree for a generational saga or costume designs for a Regency romance. But would those things have any meaning to someone who hadn't already read your book? If not, then they won't be very effective in attracting new people to your work.

The most successful reader magnet seems to be a short story or prequel work that can be read without reference to your main story. This means the people who find your reader magnet first can enjoy it as a standalone piece, rather than being lost by allusions to events that happened in other books. The purpose of the reader magnet is to give readers a sense of your writing style and introduce them to your world so that they will then choose to purchase your other work. Another way to do this is to create an extract from book 1 e.g. the first few chapters, to entice new readers. This works best when book 1 is already available to buy, or at least available on pre-order, to convert eager readers as soon as they finish the teaser. As long as the extract is less than 10% of the full book, this will not violate the exclusivity terms for Kindle Unlimited/KDP Select, if you wish to enroll your book in that program.

If you can manage it, make the reader magnet something that will appeal to people who have just read book 1, as well as to brand new readers. That way, you can use the same product for both the cookie and the magnet. (Readers who have just read all of book 1, are not going to be interested in a magnet that is the first four chapters of book 1.) A prequel novel or novelette can be teased at the end of your book 1 by saying "Want to know about Charlotte's first adventure? Find out in <prequel title>, available when you sign up to my newsletter." At the end of the prequel that you use to attract new readers, you can push the line "Want to know what happens to Charlotte after this? Find out in <book 1 title>." And thus, the same product can serve both purposes.

To be most effective your cookie or reader magnet should be something tailor-made for the series readership that you are trying to build with your mailing list. If you write standalone books all in the same genre – for example, small-town romance, or character-driven sci-fi – then a short story in that genre (but not featuring any recurring characters), which gives people an idea of your style of writing and themes, is likely to be a good hook into your work. But if you are setting up a recurring character, for example, the protagonist of an urban fantasy 6-book series, don't use some other completely unrelated story about 1920s true crime, just because you happen to have it available. Write something specific to your urban fantasy protagonist. Bring people into *that* world, so that they'll stay with you.

Because of my philosophy that the one product should serve the purpose of both finding new readers *and* enticing existing readers to join your mailing list, I tend to use the terms reader magnet and cookie interchangeably.

5.1. Distributing your reader magnet: BookFunnel

There are a few platforms you can use to distribute your reader magnet, including BookFunnel and StoryOrigin. I'm going to focus on BookFunnel because I really like it and it's the platform I know best, but the other platforms work similarly.

BookFunnel has three price plans – first-time author, mid-list author, and bestseller. If you just want to use BookFunnel to distribute your reader magnet and you only have one name that you write under, the first-time author package is sufficient. You can set up a book landing page within BookFunnel (i.e. a link from which your book can be downloaded) and join group promotions.

What you *can't* do with the first-time author package, is collect email addresses. If you want to use BookFunnel to grow your subscriber list as well as deliver your reader magnet, you will need to upgrade to at least the mid-list author plan. My advice is to use the first-time author plan while you are getting set up, and wait to upgrade until you have your onboarding sequence ready to welcome guests.

5.1.1. Uploading a book to BookFunnel

When you log in to BookFunnel, you will arrive on your home page. Any books you have already set up will be listed on this screen. Click the orange "Add New" button on the top left, and select "Add New Book" from the drop-down list. This will pull up the screen below, to enter the details of your book.

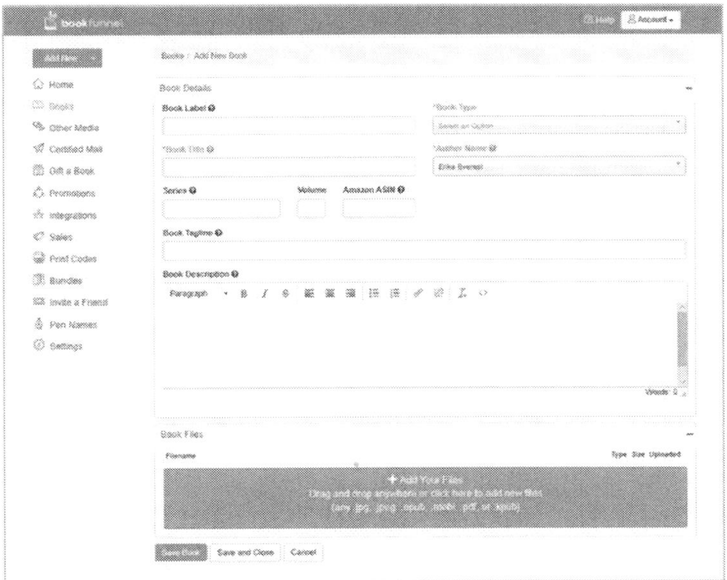

The **Book Label** is an identifier for your book that only you see. The title of your book is the simplest option – and what BookFunnel defaults to if you don't specify anything for this field. Where this field might be useful is if you have a cross-genre book and you want to use a different blurb for targeting the different genre audiences. For example, if it's a whodunnit set on a spaceship the blurb you use to entice mystery readers in a mystery & thriller promotion might be different from what you'd emphasize in a blurb targeted at space opera readers in a promotion for SFF. Identifying the different versions of your book/metadata by these distinctions in the Book Label on your book landing page may be helpful.

Book Type is a required field that identifies the type of document you are uploading (which also gives you some ideas of what can be shared via BookFunnel). The drop-down list contains Advance Copy, Excerpt, Full Book, Novella, Preview, Sample, Short Story, Teaser, Other. Select whichever type you feel fits your magnet best.

Book Title and **Author Name** are pretty self-explanatory. The **Series** and **Volume** allow you to identify if your book is part of a series, and if so, where it falls. E.g. if it is a short story set between books 3 and 4 in Series A, you could set Series = Series A and Volume = 3.5.

If you sell a book on Amazon, it will be assigned an ASIN, the Amazon Standard Identification Number. If the book you are uploading to BookFunnel is also available on Amazon, you can enter your ASIN in the **ASIN field**. This helps BookFunnel to correctly identify your book on all Kindle devices and applications. If your magnet is not for sale on Amazon, simply leave this field blank.

The **Book Description** is your blurb – the one that potential subscribers will see when they click on your book in BookFunnel. The **Book Tagline** is your hook, if you have one. Both tagline and description are optional but good to include – especially if you are joining promotions with this book.

You will need to upload the cover image as a separate file (jpeg or jpg) and the formatted content (e.g. using Vellum or Draft2Digital) in as many file types as you can e.g. mobi, epub, and pdf.

Once you have completed all the steps, save your book and close it. Your new entry should now be visible on your home screen. But this only means your book is saved within the BookFunnel system. To distribute your book, you need to create a landing page.

5.1.2. Creating a book landing page

To create a landing page, sign in to BookFunnel and click the orange "Add New" button on the top left again, but this time select "Add New Page" from the drop-down list.

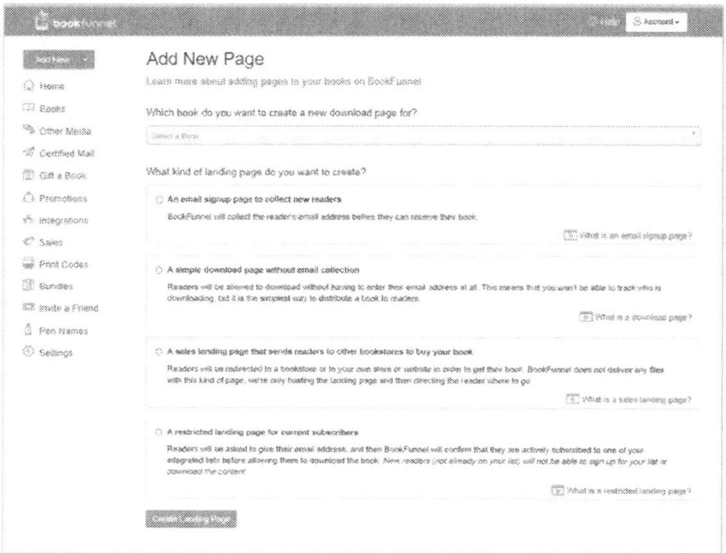

Select the book you have just uploaded from the "Select a book" drop-down list at the top. Then you need to choose which type of landing page you want. For including a link to a reader magnet in a newsletter, you want the second option here – A simple download page without email collection. (Some of these options may not be visible on the first-time author plan.)

Once you have selected your choice, click "Create Landing Page" at the bottom of the screen to bring you to the page to set up how your book will appear.

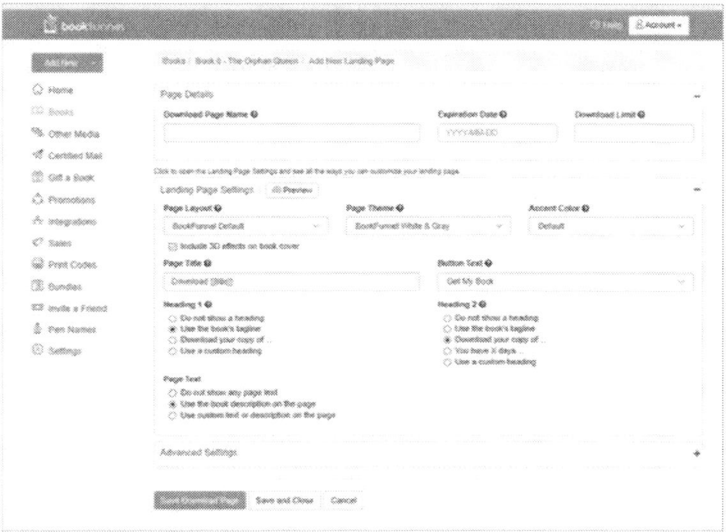

The **Download Page Name** field is a title only you will see. It helps you identify which download page you have created, especially as you may have multiple download pages per book, depending on their purpose. An example is "Series A magnet – no email collection." Readers downloading your book will see it listed by the Book Title instead (as specified on the Book page in the previous section).

For distributing your reader magnet via your newsletter, you will leave the **Expiration Date** and **Download Limit** fields blank i.e. no expiration and no limit to the total number of downloads. These might be useful for different types of landing pages e.g. distributing promotional giveaway copies, you might set the expiry as the day before your release into Kindle Unlimited, so there is no conflict with your exclusivity clause. If you are doing a giveaway but want to control how many copies are provided for free, you might set a limit of 100 copies that can be downloaded before the page stops working. Under **Advanced Settings**, you will see the standard text that a subscriber will see if the expiration or download limits have been exceeded. You can customize this text, and perhaps point them to another source for the material?

The rest of the options on this page affect the appearance of the landing page, including the appearance of your book, the color scheme, and how your blurb is presented. You can use the **Preview** button to see how each change will look. When you find a look you are happy with, finalize by clicking the orange "Save Download Page" button at the bottom.

5.2. Can I sell my magnet on Amazon?

There is no conflict between giving away a book on BookFunnel and selling it on Amazon. However, you can't be in Amazon's Kindle Select program, also known as KDP Select or Kindle Unlimited, as this requires exclusivity for the distribution of electronic copies, which distribution via BookFunnel would violate. However, as long as you are not in the KU program you can sell a BookFunnel book on Amazon as well, regardless of whether you are on other platforms also or Amazon exclusive.

Another question is about price matching. Amazon insists on price matching to other vendors so that if you have a lower price on any other platform, Amazon reserves the right to automatically lower the price of your book on Amazon to match that other price. One thing to consider in your language is that you are not giving away a book for free using BookFunnel; you are exchanging a book for the payment of an email address. Only you can determine how much that email address is worth to you. Therefore, you can set the price of your book on Amazon to whatever the value of that email address is *to you* (i.e. your compensation for not getting the email address). Instead of saying that you are selling it for a lesser price or giving it away for free, you are selling it for the price of an email address as opposed to selling it for, say, $2.99.

There are pros and cons to selling your magnet on Amazon. Exclusivity will make people more likely to sign up to the mailing list, if it's something they can't get anywhere else. However, some people never want to sign up for a marketing list but will happily pay for an item instead, and you might as well take those people's money!

If you do decide to sell your magnet as well as using it as a sign-up incentive, it's important to make sure you do not price it too cheaply. Most people would consider 99 cents a small price to pay to avoid "another set of boring emails" (of course, your emails won't be boring, but they don't know that yet). So, make the price something that will encourage them to sign up instead of purchase, if the aim of this magnet is to attract readers to your mailing list, rather than to earn you money.

6. But I don't know what to say in my emails!

Chapter Objectives

- *Assessing what topics fit your brand to include in your newsletters.*
- *Developing content to use in onboarding emails to introduce new subscribers to your newsletter and your writing.*
- *Building a template for content in your regular newsletters, using email elements described in Chapter 3.*

6.1. Onboarding sequence

My advice here is: Don't try to do everything at once. Work out what you want to say *outside of* MailerLite, such as on a word processor, so you won't need to think about the words when you are trying to work out the design and practical implementation of the sequence (which I'll cover in the next chapter.)

Write your text in Word, Google Docs, Scrivener, or whatever writing platform you prefer. Check for spelling and grammar issues (after all, this is the first impression – you want it to be a good one). Ask a friend to read over it if you aren't sure if you have the right tone. In other words, take time to get your content the way you want it before you start to build the emails themselves.

The following sections discuss in more depth about what each email should cover for a smooth onboarding sequence. Remember, there are many, many ways to do newsletters, so pick the suggestions that resonate with you.

6.1.1. Welcome and link

This is the first email that comes from *your* email address as opposed to MailerLite, so you want to create a good reputation from the start. Your reputation is enhanced when people open your emails, click on links in them, and/or reply to you – all these actions tell the email servers that people *want* your emails, and so they shouldn't be moved into spam folders.

In your welcome, thank them for signing up, remind them to whitelist you, and share the link to your cookie (BookFunnel download code) if they are meant to receive the cookie. This email will deliver almost immediately after sign-up, so can be at any hour of the day.

Don't put too much detail in this email – they have signed up, received a confirmation request, received a thank you, and now a welcome email, likely all in the space of 15 minutes. Don't ask too much! They are looking for the cookie and will be distracted until they get it. Just give it to them and wait to engage with them later.

6.1.2. Check-in

As the name suggests, this is just a way of reaching out so that you don't let too much time elapse between the first email with the cookie, and the next email when you will start your charm campaign to convert casual browsers to superfans.

Provide the link for the cookie again, in case they didn't see the first email or didn't download the cookie when they did receive the email.

If they are an organic subscriber, perhaps ask them to leave a review for whichever book led them to sign up for your list.

If you have a Facebook group (not page) where you can chat/interact with readers more directly, share the link and invite them to join you.

This shouldn't be a long email; it's just something to tide them over until you start the charm campaign in the next email.

6.1.3. First email – book inspiration

Whichever book or series your reader magnet links into, this is where you want to talk ALL about it. If it's already available, talk about the connection between the magnet and the main story (backstory, a side character, etc.) and share the link to buy the book. If it is not available, and you don't want to talk too much about the specific plot because you want to save that for when you are building to launch time, why not talk about your inspiration for the series instead? Was it a line from a song, something on the news, a conversation with a friend…? Is it something that you have been mulling over for years, or did the idea arrive fully formed in your head one day?

Where were you? Who were you with? How has the story evolved in the time since then?

By sharing why this book is special to you, you hopefully forge a connection with the reader and make it special for them as well. You want them to read on, to love your characters as much as you do. Show them why they should!

End by explaining they are part of an onboarding sequence that will last X emails at Y frequency, before being transferred to your regular mailing list e.g.

> This is the first of four emails in my onboarding sequence, introducing you to my work and inspirations. The next three emails will be sent weekly from today. After that, you will receive my monthly newsletter on the 20th of each month.

6.1.4. General topics – genre chats

But I don't have any books written yet! I hear you cry. *What am I meant to talk about??*

I was the same – I started my mailing list before my books were ready to release (I was stockpiling the first three titles for rapid release). I didn't want to talk about the books too much, in case it diluted the impact when I was ready to build to launch, but I wanted to start a platform so I would have people to launch to.

I decided to talk to my subscribers as if I was meeting them at a genre fan convention. What topics would you talk about if you met a kindred soul who loves the books you love for the same reasons? I write fairy tales, so I talked (okay, ranted) about the passive princess trope in classic/original versions and in some Disney adaptations.

For YA (young adult) dystopian, you could discuss whether the love triangle trope enhances the story or dilutes the message.

For Science Fiction, 20 reasons they shouldn't have canceled Firefly.

For Romance, have the Billionaires worn out their welcome?

You know your genre best – why did you decide to write the story you did? What books or films inspired you, and which ones made you grind your teeth? Talk about your reactions and say why: you'll probably find the people who share your views are the ones most likely to enjoy your stories!

Ask for your subscribers' opinions too. If you can get them to reply, you have a chance to build a much more personal connection with them. But remember to avoid topics that are 'current' such as the new Marvel film – the onboarding sequence is planned to run forever (or at least for a few months) so you don't want something you have to constantly tweak to avoid it looking out of date.

6.1.5. Other series/books to promote

If you have written books or series not connected to your reader magnet series, you should also draw attention to those in your introduction. This assumes, of course, that they are for a similar readership – don't promote erotica to your Christian Inspiration readers.

If you don't have the magnet series buy or pre-order links available yet, you might want to include these other books in the First Email, where you introduce your work. Otherwise, have it as a later email in the chain. Don't put it right after the First Email though – you don't want too many "buy my book" emails upfront. Remember the give-ask ratio. Try to give some value to the subscriber while asking for nothing in an email (e.g. one of those genre questions) before introducing your other work.

If you have a large back catalog, this may not be feasible. In that case, I recommend that at the end of the First Email that you say how many series the forthcoming emails will introduce them to. I would also suggest focusing traffic to first-in-series books only, saying how many books are in each series currently, and whether the series is complete (and if it's not, how often new installments will be released).

If you plan to present multiple series in the same newsletter, you may want to change the emphasis of these "additional series" emails to give them more weight. But remember to put the series linked to the reader magnet first – because that's what brought this subscriber into your funnel.

6.2. Regular mailings

Now that we've got your onboarding sequence set up, let's have a look at what you can discuss in your regular emails. Depending on how many sections you have, you may want to start with a brief introduction, summarizing what will be in the newsletter. E.g.

> In today's newsletter, I finally have a title to share with you for my work-in-progress, book 3 of the XXX series, an update on how Fluffy is coping after her vet visit I told you about last month, and some great new releases and special offers, including the new YYY book by ZZZ. If you haven't read this series yet, you're going to love it!

6.2.1. Book news/writing progress

Release dates, cover reveals, snippets, writing prompts, or just how many chapters/scenes you wrote this week (authors love word counts but it isn't as meaningful to readers) – tell them how you are doing.

If your books require research – scientific discoveries, poisons of the Victorian era, political hierarchy in small African nations – share what your sources are and interesting discoveries along the way. Even if they don't make it into the book, readers who like your work will probably like seeing "behind the scenes" and how it comes together.

If you have any in-person appearances coming up – conventions, bookstore readings, fan meet-ups – let them know. Did a book club use your book as their pick of the week? Celebrate! (And doubly so if you were able to connect with them for a post-reading discussion with the author via Skype or Zoom!)

6.2.2. Personal stories

This is the part that most people balk at. Sure, if you're comfortable talking about your spouse, two children, and three dogs, go for it. But if you're not, that's okay too. Personal can be as deep or shallow as you want, as long as it's *real.*

Pets can be a great source of personal connection without being too intrusive. If you have a pet, share photos and stories about them, and invite your readers to share their fur-babies with you too. It generally gets a good response. But if you don't have a pet, maybe you could have an imaginary pet? Oh, I don't mean lie! But, for example...

> I always wanted a dog but my husband is allergic to them, so we can't. If I were to get a dog, I think I'd go for either a cocker spaniel or maybe a chow-chow. There's a lovely labradoodle called Trixie that has her own YouTube channel. I pretend Trixie is my dog, and watch her videos to get my little doggie fixes every day.

People will start to associate chow-chows, labradoodles, and/or cocker spaniels with you and will think of you when they see one. If they have one of their own, they might send you pictures. It creates a connection, and that's what it's all about.

Cozy mysteries (and other cozies) are often linked around a craft – like baking, knitting, or gardening. Chances are that if you are writing about this, you are interested in and knowledgeable about it too. So, share your recipes/patterns/gripes about weevils, and also photos of the finished pieces – whether they work as intended or not! Find other people who share your passions and *connect with them.*

David Gaughran always mentions which music he is currently listening to at the end of his weekly email, and I know of another author who creates writing playlists on Spotify and shares them with her subscribers.

But remember to keep it relevant to your writing! One author shares her celebrity crush on Jason Momoa (and her fans respond with the latest memes and pictures of the actor) which suits her steamy romance audience. But if your passion is Japanese horror movies, talking about it may put off your sweet romance readers!

Finally, it must be *real*. Don't say you always wanted a dog if, in fact, you hate dogs. Don't claim fabulous baking skills if you struggle to boil water. People will spot a fake, and there is no quicker way of alienating a group than trying to bluff your way through something they are passionate and knowledgeable about.

6.2.3. Newsletter swaps/group promos

If you are looking to grow your subscribers, there are many promotions you can participate in on platforms such as BookFunnel and StoryOrigin. To participate, you will need to share something with your own subscribers – usually a link to the promotion and the other books in it: this is the part of your newsletter where you can do that.

Getting other authors in your genre to share your book with their readers is a great way to grow your readership. This is known as a newsletter swap, but, as the name suggests, you need to reciprocate. In this section, you can include links to other authors' new releases and special offers. Consider how many you can realistically feature each newsletter – at what point will your readers get fatigued? Also, the further down on a list a book is featured, the fewer eyes that will see it. In fairness to other authors, if you are sharing their work make sure they have a good chance of being seen. Also, too many links to other authors can make your newsletter seem like an advertising brochure. This will likely increase your unsubscribe numbers, which in turn damages your overall deliverability.

What you include with a shared book is a personal decision, but there are a few things to consider. If you include the full book description with each book shared, this can increase the length of your newsletter very quickly. If you already have a lot of content in the previous sections, this might be overwhelming or off-putting for your reader. You could summarize the blurb yourself, or just select the hook to include, but consider that whatever you start with, you will have to maintain to show consistency. Having to customize the text for other authors' books may take more time than you have to give to the process. At a minimum, include the reason you have been asked to share *this* book – usually that will be because it is a new release or on sale. E.g.

- **New release:** <Title>, the latest installment in the <Series title> by <author name>, has just been released. Get your copy at <links>.
- **Sale:** The <Series title> Complete Omnibus by <author name> is on special offer – only $4.99 for all six books until Friday 10th. Get your copy at <links>.

If you have read the book yourself, or other books by the author, you may want to say something more about the book. In this case, I would suggest listing it as a "personal recommendation" as described in the next section.

When you launch your book, you'll want as many other authors in your genre to share your new release. But if you are restricting the number of books that you will promote in a single newsletter this may feel like a limit to what you can ask for your book in return. A way around this is to build up a list of shares earlier, in the months before your launch. Then you will have lots of people ready to return the mention, without being constrained by the contemporaneous space you can offer. (Plus, you probably won't want to share any other books during your own launch week, to make sure all attention is on *your* book!)

6.2.4. Personal Recommendations

This is another version of sharing other author's books, but this focuses on books you have read, enjoyed, and would be a good fit with your genre/readership. For these, you can introduce them with your own reasons why you think your readers would enjoy the book, rather than just sharing the standard blurb (book description). A personal recommendation helps the reader find a new book to read while waiting for your next one.

You might want to put this section before the newsletter swaps book shares, as this is your curated list of books you know will be a good fit. Good recommendations build trust between you and your readers, so you will need to be judicious about what you include. By comparison, you may not know the authors you do swaps with, other than that they are in your genre. You can't read every book before including it in your newsletter, so you may find it helpful to draw this distinction between the sections.

If you see a boxset coming out for books you have already read and enjoyed, it is a great opportunity to get share a relevant book in your genre in a more personal way while simultaneously gaining goodwill from another author for sharing their newly released boxset with your readers.

Ultimately, a personal recommendation is with the reader in mind. While the reader may find a bargain or a new favorite in your newsletter swaps, the reality is that those shares are more for you the author, to aid in publicity for your own books, than for enhancing your readers' experiences.

7. Building the onboarding sequence

Chapter Objectives

- *Combining the content from Chapter 6 with the template in Chapter 3 to create compelling emails.*
- *Utilizing the workflow elements from Chapter 4 to build a set-it-and-forget-it onboarding sequence with these emails.*
- *Leveraging MailerLite features to funnel multiple starting points into the same final sequence, to minimize rework.*

All automation sequences are triggered by **joining** (assigning subscribers to) a specific group. For the sake of clarity, we'll call that group ONBOARDING. So, the first step in the sequence will be "When subscriber joins ONBOARDING."

I suggest adding a **delay** of 1 minute next. This is because you will assign subscribers to multiple groups at once, and in case there is any delay between them, you want to ensure all other groups are established before the next step.

The next step is a **condition** – Cookie or No Cookie? Who gets the cookie (reader magnet) is determined by another group/tag: DELIVERCOOKIE. So, the third step is a Condition Group Membership: DELIVERCOOKIE, with outcomes YES (green thumbs up) and NO (red thumbs down).

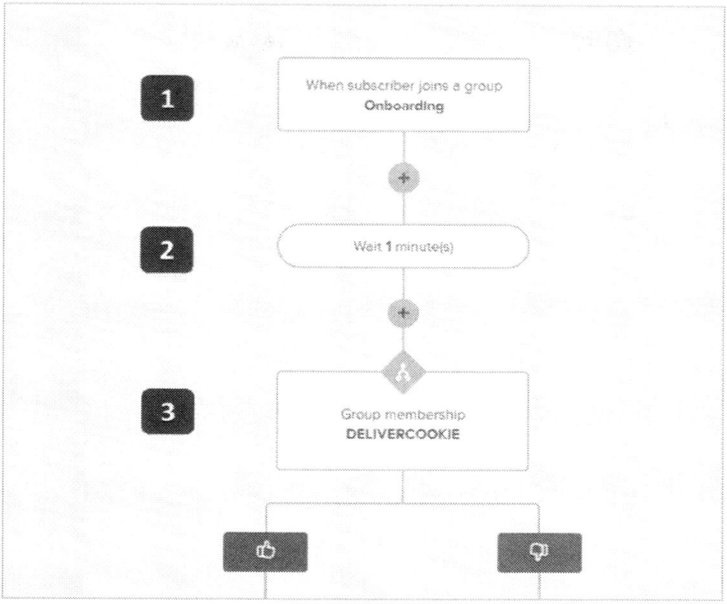

We will look at what comes next for each of these outcomes separately, starting with YES.

7.1. Onboarding sequence with cookie

Step 4 is an **email**, specifically your welcome email. In this, you thank them for signing up, remind them to whitelist you, and share the link to your magnet (BookFunnel download code). This email will deliver almost immediately after sign-up, so can be at any hour of the day.

Step 5 is another **delay**. Give them some time to read the magnet, then check-in. I suggest 2 days.

Step 6 is the check-in **email**. Ask if they got the book. Give them the link again in case not. Remind them of the BookFunnel support team for technical challenges. Tell them when you will contact them again.

Step 7 is another **delay**. There are two options here, depending on how you manage your emails.

1. You can have a short onboarding sequence and then drop the subscribers onto your main mailing list, OR
2. You can make your regular emails part of the sequence so that everyone gets the same emails in the same order, but not at the same time.

For option 1, the delay should be an interval appropriate to the interval for your regular schedule e.g. if regular newsletters go out once a month, then perhaps once a week to build initial engagement. If you will be sending your newsletter every two weeks, then maybe 2-3 days between the mails in the onboarding sequence. But also consider the content of these emails: if you are pointing them to another series or two, you need to give them time to read without bombarding them!

For option 2, the delay should be until the day of the week/month that your regular mailing goes out on. Once they are on this schedule, it is easy to maintain.

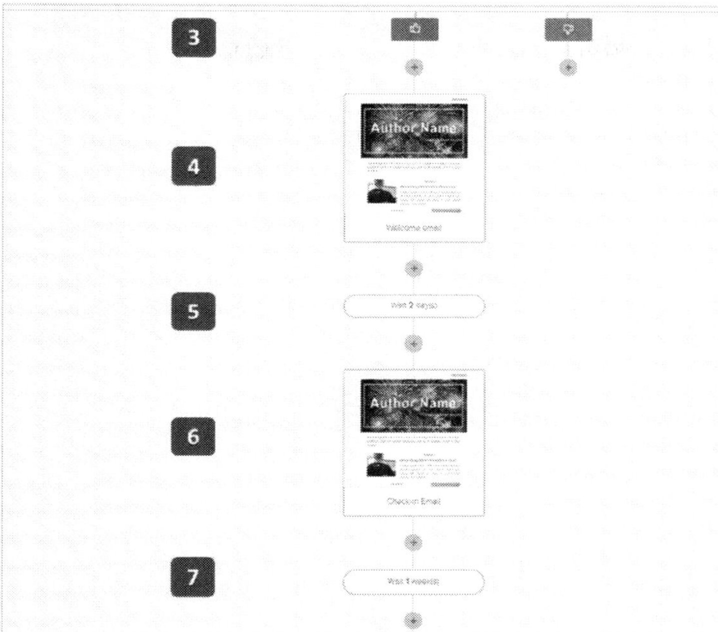

Step 8 is another **email**. Specifically, this is the "First email" described in Section 6.1.3 where you discuss the inspiration for your book/series.

Step 9: Repeat steps 7 (**delay**) and 8 (**email**) until your onboarding is complete. This may be just one more email, or several, depending on what you'd like to tell your readers (suggestions for this part are in Section 6.1.4 and 6.1.5). For the last line of the final email in the onboarding sequence, state that they have completed the sequence, will now join your main list, and when and how often they can expect to hear from you.

Step 10 is an **action** to move or copy them to the group that will be used for your regular mailings. Let's call this group REGULAR. So, the action step will be *Copy to group* >

REGULAR (or *Move to group* > REGULAR, if you don't want them to remain on your onboarding list).

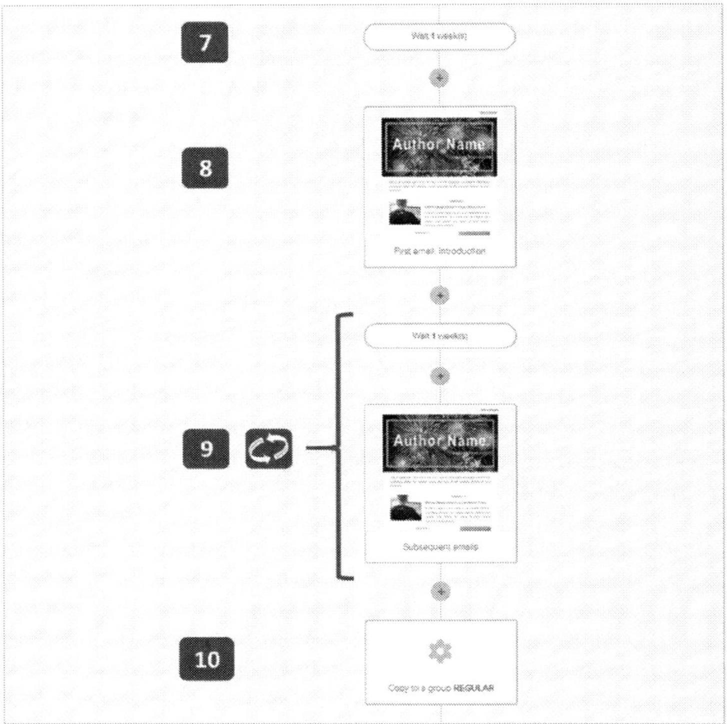

7.2. Onboarding sequence without cookie

Let's go back to Step 3, and look at the other branch of that condition – those for whom Condition Group Membership: DELIVERCOOKIE outcome is NO.

Why would you *not* want to give someone your magnet/cookie? Well, if someone joined your mailing list as part of a promo where they had *already* received your cookie, then sending it again is both redundant and potentially irritating. How you approach the content of these emails is different than for the cookie-delivery folks. They may be signed up to multiple author email lists – how do you engage them to make sure they not only stay on *your* list, but gradually convert to superfans too?

Step 11: My recommendation is that the first **email** you send them combines some of the generic welcome text from the email in Step 4, and some of the series-specific details in Step 8. I also suggest that you start with "You joined my mailing list when you downloaded my book <magnet title> as part of a BookFunnel promotion last week/month/etc." You may want to specify the name of the promotion, but that is another layer of tagging and customization, so I suggest you don't bother. Also, insert a picture of your reader magnet book cover – this will remind them more than the title which book was yours (and prompt them to read it, if they haven't already). If the book that follows on from your magnet is available, this might be a good time to mention it and share its order links.

This is where we get clever. Instead of writing a whole new sequence for non-cookie subscribers, we are going to leverage what is already written from Step 9. Thus, Step 12 is an **action** step, redirecting the workflow to connect up with the existing emails you wrote for the cookie subscribers. Action = Move to another Step > Filter by Step = Delay > select the appropriate delay (the one before the first email in Step 9 – don't use the email in Step 8, because you have already recycled this text to make your non-cookie welcome email.)

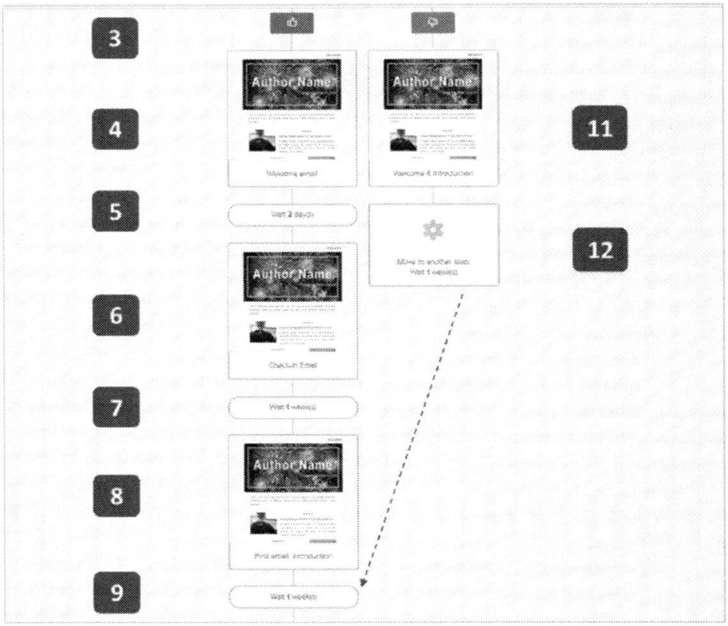

This is the end of the non-cookie workflow. These subscribers will follow steps 9 and 10 and be added to your REGULAR group for standard delivery. However, they will not have the tag DELIVERCOOKIE and *will* have the tag SIGNUP-BOOKFUNNEL (or whatever source they came from), so you can continue to identify them in the future.

7.3. Onboarding sequence for organic subscribers

An organic subscriber is one who signs up to your mailing list *after* they have read your work, often from a link in your backmatter. These people are precious, so value them and treat them well. How you talk to them is different from how you talk to other subscribers – they already know you, and they like you enough to have asked for more when they finished!

This is where having different sign-up links for every location becomes really important – because you can tell which book prompted them to join, and you know how far they have read in your series so you can say things without worrying about spoilers. This creates an immediate connection with these subscribers, which makes it so much easier to talk to them (and to sell to them later!)

To have a different set of steps for organic subscribers, you first need to separate these subscribers in the workflow. You do this by adding a new condition to the workflow. Because these organic subscribers will want to receive the reader magnet/cookie, they should be under the YES branch of that condition (Step 3). Thus, Step 13 is a new **condition** inserted after Step 3, on the positive branch, asking whether the subscriber is a member of the Organic group. When inserting a condition, you are asked where the existing subsequent steps should be moved to: YES or NO. Move the existing welcome sequence for non-organic subscribers to the NO branch.

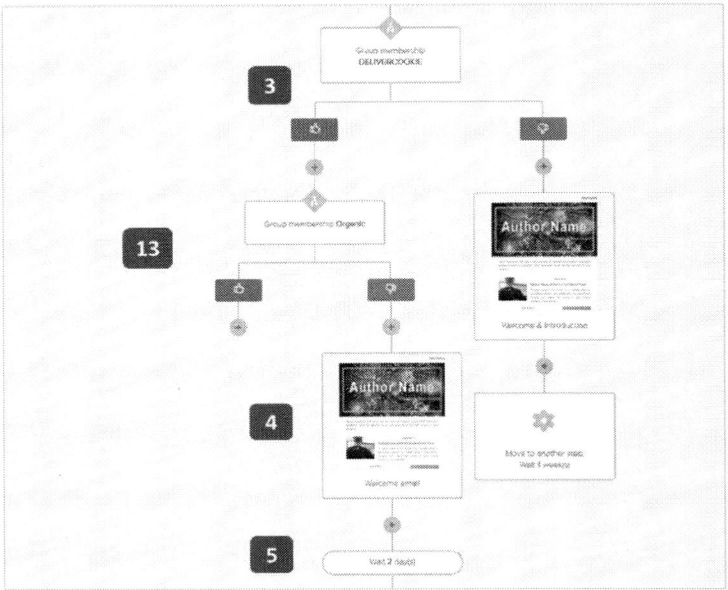

The rest of the organic onboarding sequence is added under the YES branch of the condition in Step 13.

Step 14 is the organic welcome **email**. It has all the same stuff as Step 4, but it starts with an acknowledgment that they have read your book e.g. "Thank you so much for reading <book title> and for now signing up to my newsletter. I guess if you are here you must have liked the book!" Then provide them with the links for the magnet they signed up for, as per Step 4.

Step 15: a **delay**, as per Step 5.

Step 16: a check-in **email**, as per Step 6. Ask if they enjoyed the cookie, then ask them to post a review of the book that brought them to your list (you will know this name from your tagging of the Sign-up Source). E.g. "Would you consider leaving a review on Amazon or Goodreads <another

platform>? Reviews are so important in helping new readers decide if a series is something that they want to invest their time and money in, and we authors really appreciate it."

Step 17: a **delay**, as per Step 7.

Step 18 is the first **email** in the sequence. You can't use the same email as in Step 8, because you know these subscribers have read at least one of your books already. If they have read book 1, perhaps ask if they are aware of books 2, 3, etc.? If they joined from a later book in the series (and it is possible to read the series out of order), perhaps ask if they are aware of book 1 and point them to it. If the next book in your series is not available yet, perhaps tell them that you are working on it and a few allusions to what comes next in the story (building on the knowledge you *know* they have from reading your existing books.)

Step 19 is a repeat of Step 12, an **action** to move these organic subscribers to pick up the remaining onboarding delays/emails that the non-organic subscribers are getting.

3
13
14
15
16
17
18
19
Author Name

The complete workflow, with all options and branches, will look like this:

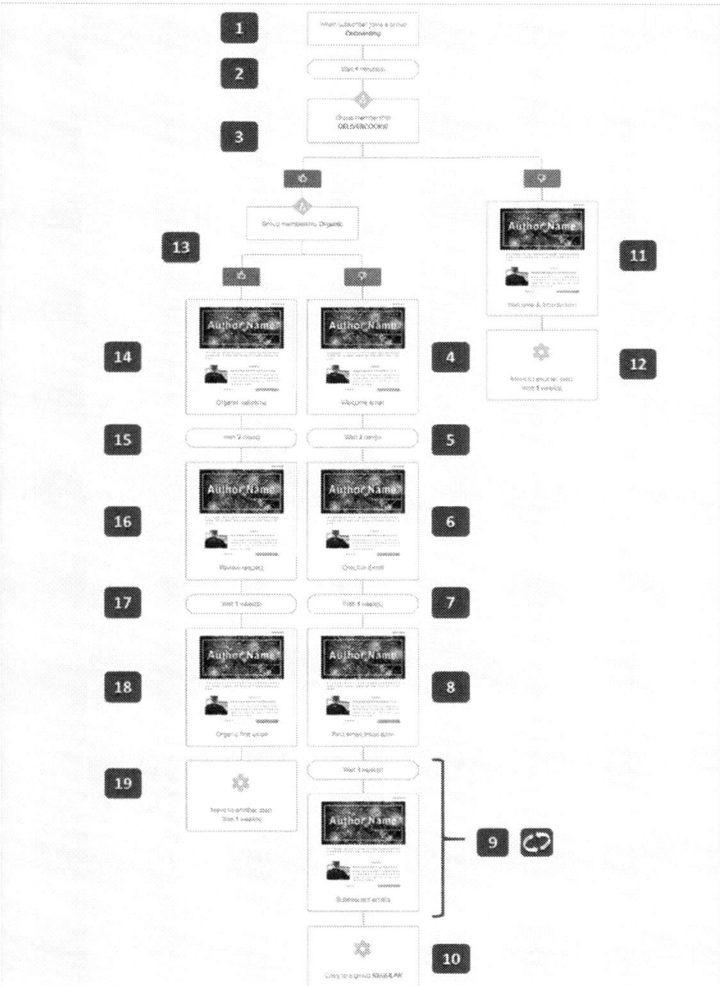

8. Signing up

Chapter Objectives

- *Knowing the difference between landing pages and embedded forms, and when to use each for collecting new subscribers.*
- *Wording the sign-up text to be compliant with GDPR rules.*
- *Wording the success message and double opt-in emails to ensure subscribers make it onto your list.*
- *Assessing what subscriber information to collect at sign-up, and what to leave until later.*
- *Learning how to update subscriber information after sign-up, to collect that extra information.*

8.1. Landing pages

To create a space where you can collect sign-ups from new subscribers, go first to **Sites** on the green ribbon at the top of the screen, and then select **Landing page**. Select the orange "create new landing page" button. You will be prompted to enter a name for your landing page. I suggest you consider linking the name to where you will use this link, e.g. "Sign up page for Facebook." I'm simply calling this "strategic author."

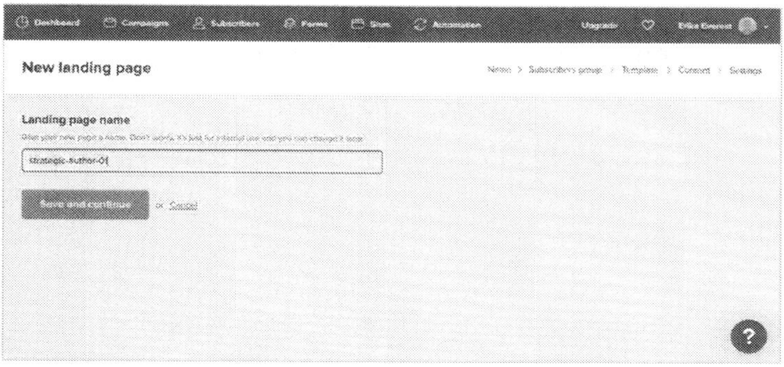

When you continue, you get a choice of template to use as a starting point for building your landing page. There are over 30 templates available at present, with more added regularly. My recommendation is to build your own, much as we built the newsletter ourselves rather than using preformatted templates. This is because many of the existing templates for landing pages are salesy – they are explaining *why* a subscriber would want to sign up. In our world, we've already convinced them to sign up; this is just how they do it. So better to keep it simple with less to distract them from giving us their email address and permission to contact them.

So, pick any template and, when you select it, you will be brought to the template editor. This is similar in concept to the email editor, though slightly different in layout. In the black ribbon along the top, go to Actions and "remove content blocks" as we did before. This erases everything from the template (which is why it doesn't matter which template you choose) and allows us to start from scratch with a layout that suits us.

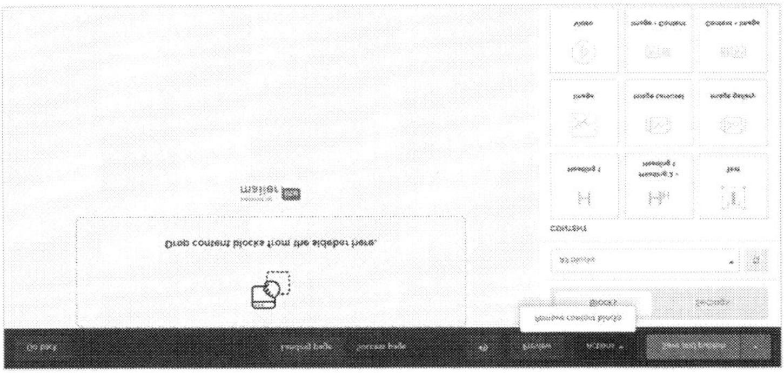

On the right-hand side, you can see the list of blocks, similar to the email drag-and-drop builder. The first blocks we need to consider are in the sub-list for **Forms**. There are 3 types of forms: the Signup form, the Simple signup form, and the Contact form. For our purposes, I believe the Simple signup form is closest to what we're trying to achieve. Select this block, drag it to your template, and we'll get started.

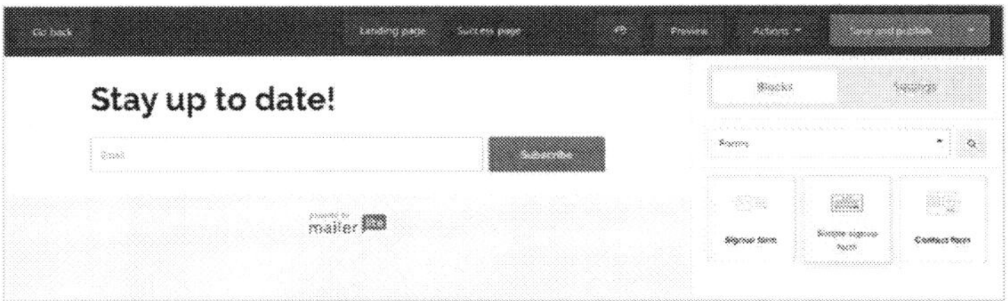

On the Content tab, you can enter a heading for your newsletter and a description of what you are asking them to sign up for. Here, I've kept it simple: "join my newsletter" is a pretty self-explanatory title. But you might want to be so do something a little more creative. "Are you ready to explore the stars?" if you're writing space opera or intergalactic sci-fi, or "Time to get your spell books out" for a paranormal academy.

The text for your description is important. It's not just one last chance to encourage them to sign up; it is your contract with your reader. If you say "I'll email you updates on new releases" then you can't send them cat memes every Tuesday. You need to be clear that it is the newsletter they are signing up for: don't say "give me your email address to receive a free book" and then send them your newsletter. Tell them "join my newsletter and, when you do, you can get this free book" instead. The important aspect is that they are choosing to join the newsletter list and that by giving you their email address they are consenting, knowledgeably and explicitly, to that. Include the frequency at which you will be sending emails, and remind them that they can unsubscribe at any time.

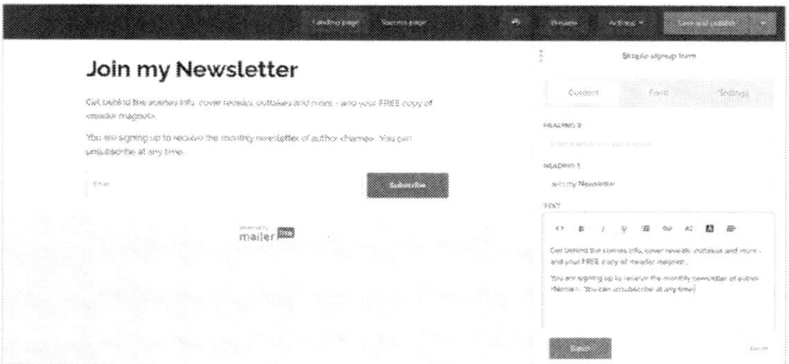

Moving to the **Form** tab, we can insert the fields that we are collecting. **Email** is a required field. For the personalization reasons I discussed before, I always like to collect **Name**, and I also collect **Last name** as an optional field. The reason I collect Last name is twofold: one, it helps me identify and track individual subscribers if I meet them on Facebook or other settings. Secondly, I wanted to be clear that the Name field is not your whole name. If you are just asked for your name, you could respond James P Sullivan, and saying "Hello James P Sullivan" at the start of every email doesn't feel very personal. "Hello James" works a bit better. By including Last name, it clarifies that Name is just what the subscriber wishes to be addressed as, which is the purpose for which we wish to use that field.

As you can see, it is possible to modify the text that appears for each of these field labels, whereas the field name itself is a set term based on the personalized fields we spoke about earlier. I change my labels to include an asterisk for the required items, and explicitly state 'optional' for the rest. You can see that there is a checkbox under the label saying this field is required. If you tick it, the field is mandatory, if you don't it's optional.

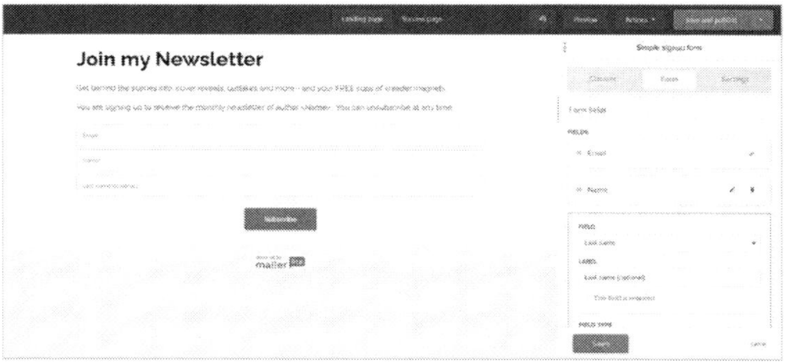

So now that the three fields are on my newsletter, I save that and scroll down to click the button to "Show labels above input" rather than in the boxes. This is just a personal choice, so pick whichever suits you best. You can also see the button to add further fields to your form, for other information you wish to collect at sign-up.

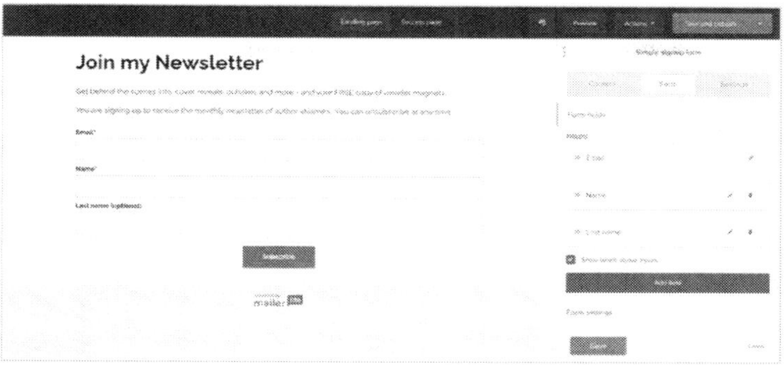

Moving down to the **Form settings** on the same tab, there are some other items that you can include as part of your sign-up. Confirmation checkbox and Marketing permission fields are about being compliant with GDPR. You don't need either of them if you have specified your description correctly. If you've outlined the purpose for which you will be using their information then they have already given consent, and because we are using double opt-in there will be a confirmation of this in a moment.

Interest groups allow your subscriber to self-select which tags they will have. **Hidden segmentation field** applies tags of your choosing based on their sign up. As we've discussed before, I prefer to do the segmentation/tagging via the group membership and therefore ignore these terms.

One thing I do like to add is a reCAPTCHA option. It reduces spam and bots trying to sign up to your newsletter, and thus makes life a little bit easier.

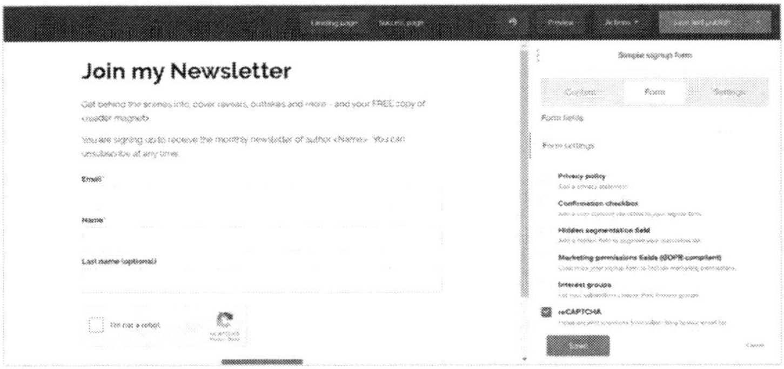

Moving back to the **Contents** sub-list of blocks, select the image and put it at the top of the sign-up form.

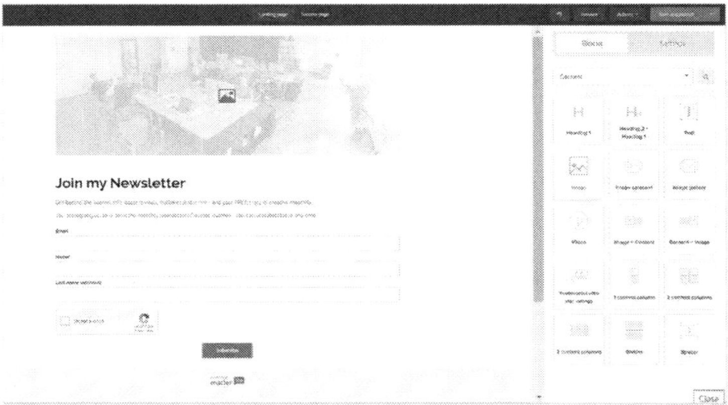

As before, we use our consistent branding image to go on top of the form, adjusting the alignment, size, etc., as we have done before.

Finally, if you go back to the **Settings** tab, you can change the colors of the background, the button, and everything else, as you want. Here is an example.

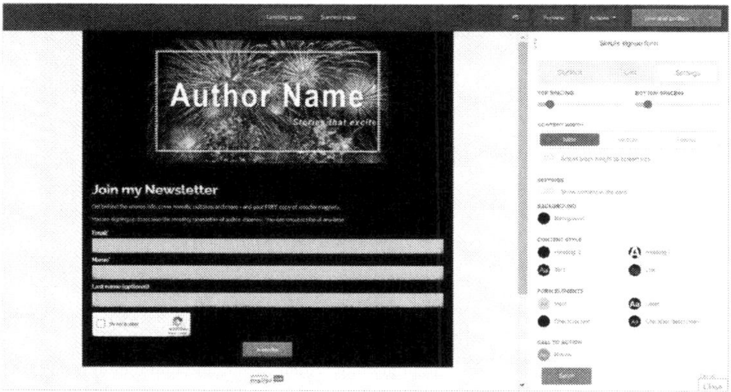

Of course, you could do this at the start when you're editing the form the first time, but for me, it was easier to wait until I had the picture in place to pick up those colors and make sure that everything would look well together. However, if you have a very clear vision of what you want, it may make sense to do it all at once when you add the simple signup form block, and that's fine too.

8.1.1. Success page

The success page is what appears to your subscriber after they click "subscribe." This will be a confirmation "yay, you're signed up" – or at least, that's the default text that MailerLite often shows.

To get to the success page so we can edit it ourselves, select **Success page** on the black bar at the top. This will bring you into a new form, though still within the landing page set up. Again, "remove all blocks" via the Actions, and assign a text block instead. You may wish to include your banner on this page – or perhaps not, depending on how obvious you want your message to be. The message you need to give is:

Please check your inbox for your confirmation email. Remember to check Spam and promotion folders as well, as it may have gone to those sections. You will need to click on the confirmation email before you are subscribed to the list.

This last part is because of the double-opt-in requirement of GDPR which we'll talk about in a moment.

Another important thing to put into your success email, as well as reminding them to check Spam and promotions, is to ask them to whitelist your author email. (Your author email is the one you use to send mails in MailerLite; whatever you signed up to your MailerLite account with and the name that appears in your "from" field. In my case it's Erika@erikaeverest.com.) **Whitelisting** means that your email address will automatically go to the primary folder. You can also refer to this as adding to contacts. Asking them to do this now means they're more likely to take that action and thereby receive future emails from you. The process for whitelisting is different depending on the email provider, web browser, and many other factors. Thus, rather than trying to explain how-to for each of these combinations – and being subject to providing Tech Support thereafter – they can Google the term instead and find the instructions relevant for them.

Finally, check your preview mode for both desktop and mobile for your success page and your landing page and, once you are happy with everything, click "save and continue" to move to the next step: the settings for your landing page.

8.1.2. Page settings: sign-up link and other details

The most important part of the page settings for me is the Landing page URL i.e. your sign-up link. You can only specify a custom domain (e.g. your website) in the paid package for MailerLite. However, this does not mean that you have to have a generic subscription link if you are on the free plan.

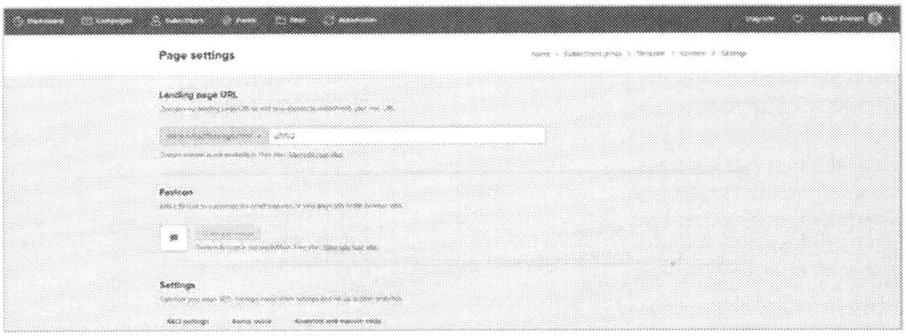

MailerLite uses subscribepage.com and assigns 6 characters by default as your unique link code, but you can change the code to anything you want. My preference has been my name followed by a dash and the location where the sign-up occurs, so Erika Everest-Facebook, Erika Everest-Amazon, etc.

Subscribepage.com isn't so explicit that it shouts you are using the free product (unless people already know it, in which case they're probably not your standard reader.) Including your name makes it personal (and more memorable for the subscriber, if they have to retype it.) Including the source is just a way to help you differentiate the sign-up links for different locations.

Favicon is the picture that appears beside the page name on the tab in your web browser. The image below shows the favicons for Google, Facebook, MailerLite, and Amazon, as examples.

By default, the favicon for your landing page is the MailerLite speech bubble. Changing the icon is not available as an option in the free package, so we can ignore it for now.

Most of the rest of the Page settings are dedicated to **SEO – Search engine optimization**. This includes metadata for your landing page, such as what appears in the ribbon at the top describing your page (Page title) and also some aspects that could be searched for, if you were to include it in a Google search.

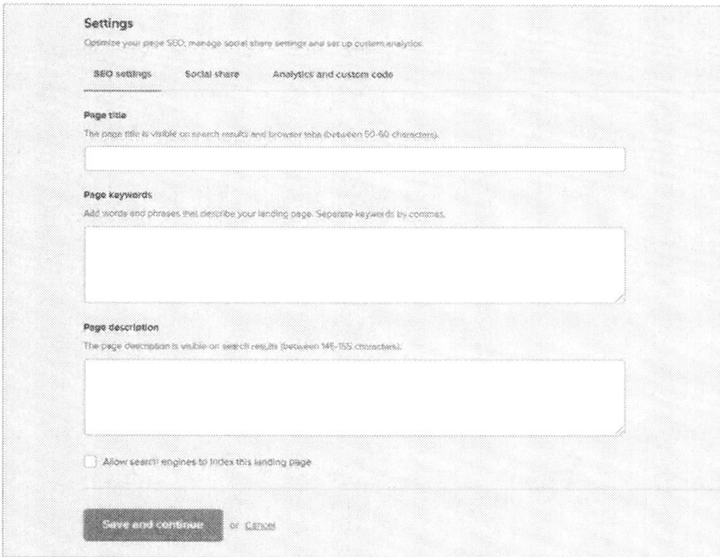

SEO is a huge topic, and outside the scope of this book. Personally, I am not looking for people to search for my landing page. I intend to give the link to the relevant people so that I can more easily identify where they have come from (Facebook ad, newsletter swap, etc.) People doing a Google search should find my website or my Facebook author page, not a random sign-up form. Thus, SEO is not something I worry about overly much, and just put in high-level descriptive detail for the page name and specify that this is an author newsletter sign-up page.

8.2. Double opt-in

At the top of the summary page, you will see a button for double opt-in marked as off. Always, *always* turn this on. Not only is double opt-in a requirement of GDPR (the EU privacy regulations), it's also an efficient way to make sure you've only got people who really want to be on your list. If they go to the effort of confirming their subscription, they're more likely to stick with you after that. This also eliminates invalid email addresses from being added to your active subscribers list, which would negatively impact your deliverability rates.

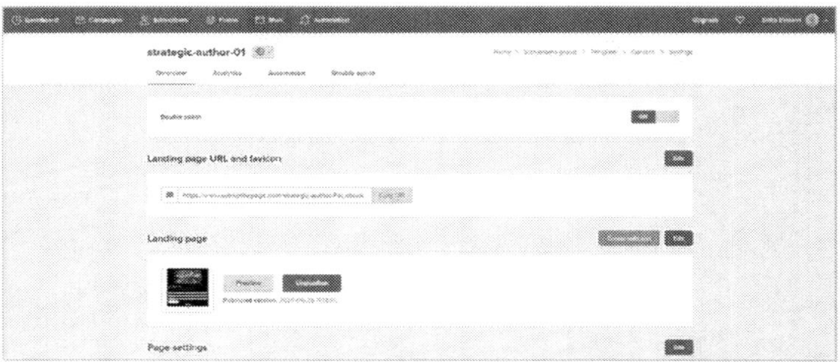

When you turn double opt-in on a new Option appears at the top of the summary page: the double opt-in option. If you click on this you will find two templates. Unlike with the landing page, these templates are not a page; these are emails.

8.2.1. Confirmation

The first email is the **confirmation email**. This basically says "this email address has attempted to sign up to our list. Is that you? Did you mean to?" and if they click the button to indicate "yes," they will be added to your list. Until they click that button, they will *not* be subscribed. This confirmation email will often end up in a spam folder, promotions folder, or other hidden-away places within whatever email provider they use. This is why it is so, SO important when you are creating the success page associated with your landing page that you remind them to check these locations to find this confirmation email. There is default text provided by MailerLite as you can see here.

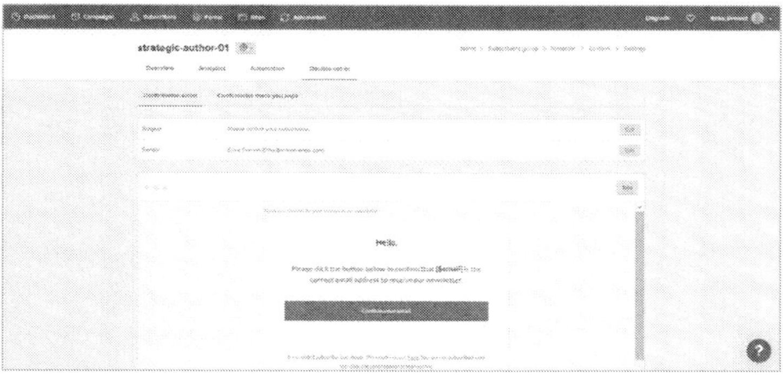

You may wish to customize this and that is also fine as long as you keep in the critical elements of:

- confirming the email address,
- the opt-in button,
- explaining again what they are opting in for i.e. the monthly newsletter for author <name>, and
- Reminding them of the whitelisting instructions i.e. add me to your contacts.

If they have just had to go rooting in various sub-folders to find where your email ended up, then this is the time they are most likely to want to make sure your emails end up in their inbox in the future. So, remind them of your email address and that they need to whitelist it.

To customize the appearance of the confirmation email, use the **Edit** button above the preview. This opens the email editor so you can drag-and-drop the required blocks to create a confirmation email aligned with your branding.

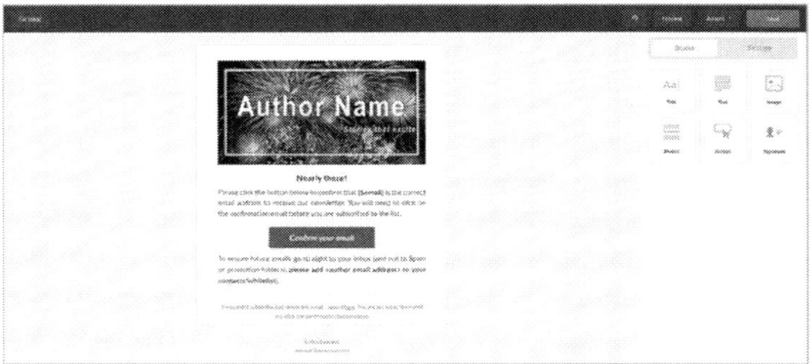

8.2.2. Thank you

The thank-you email automatically sends when they click be subscribe button, and it just says "thank you; you are now subscribed to the newsletter."

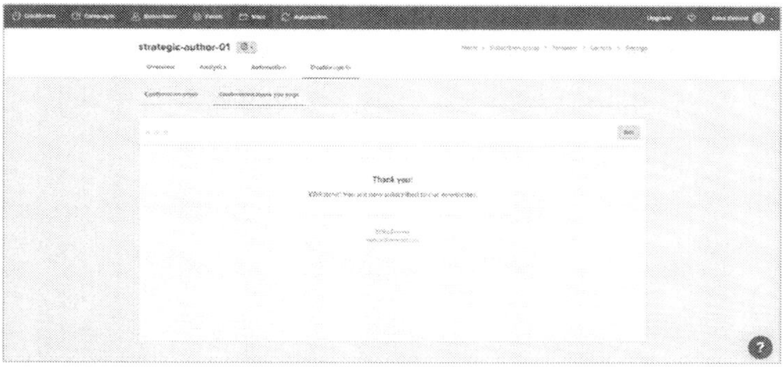

I've seen that some people use the Thank You email to send the reader magnet to the subscriber. This is because this is the first email that you're sending the subscriber after they have definitely confirmed they want to be on your list, so why not give them what they've signed on for?

The answer to that is deliverability. These confirmation and thank you emails are still part of MailerLite's server. You want the first email they get to be from *you*, from *your* email, and not from a generic MailerLite server. This makes a difference because if it's coming from you it contributes to your sender reputation. The better your reputation, the more likely future emails from you will end up in the main inbox and not those other subfolders, and that, of course, is what we're aiming for. Not everyone will whitelist you, but if the people who interact with your emails do so positively it increases your sender reputation and informs providers and servers that your content is generally to be trusted and should be delivered to the inbox. Positive interactions include opens, link clicks, and replies. The email with the reader magnet is the most likely to be both opened and clicked, and you want those positive interactions associated with *your* email address and sender reputation.

Therefore, use the thank you email to simply say thank you, confirm that they're signed up, and tell them that their welcome email with their free reader magnet should be arriving in their inbox in a few moments. And again, remind them to whitelist to make sure it goes straight to the inbox. As with the confirmation email, you can manage the email appearance by clicking the Edit button to bring you to the email editor.

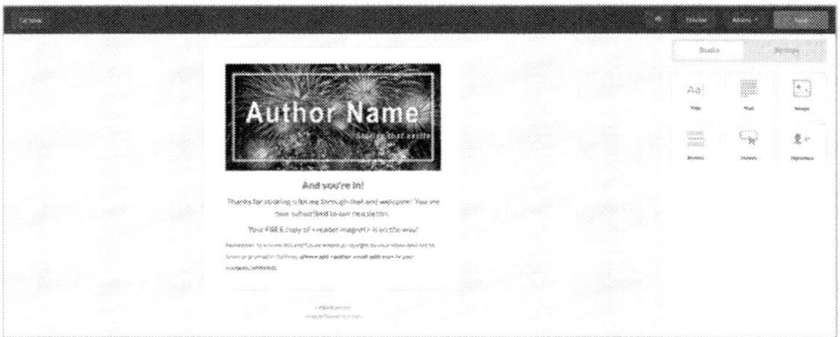

And that completes the sign-up process using a landing page.

8.3. Embedded forms

Embedded forms are designed to be an insert on your website rather than a page in themselves. As a result, they are much simpler in design. To create an embedded form, go to the **Forms** tab on the green ribbon. There are 3 sections within the Forms tab:

- Pop-ups
- Embedded forms
- Promotions

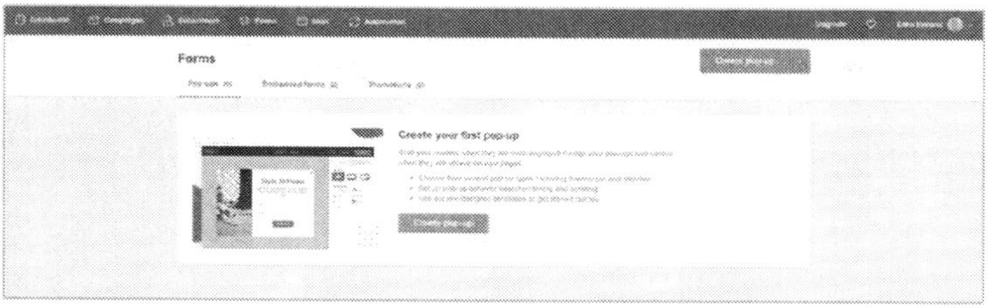

Pop-ups are sign-up forms that appear on screen after a certain amount of time scrolling/viewing has elapsed. Promotions are pop-ups also, but designed for a special offer or other information that you want to grab attention. Personally, I find pop-ups invasive and annoying. I know you may have a different opinion, but in the context of my super-simplistic website, I don't expect any traffic to arrive there unless they were already looking for me. In which case, I would prefer the sign-up link to be immediately visible, rather than waiting for the pop-up to appear. Many potential readers also use pop-up blockers. Which brings us to embedded forms.

To build a new form, select the orange **Create embedded form** button at the top of the Embedded forms section. As with the landing page, you need to give your form a name.

Once you've done that, you'll be asked to select which of your existing groups a subscriber should be added to when they sign up using this form. If you don't already have one, create a new group. I would suggest using SIGNUP-WEBSITE for this form, as it is likely to be only used for your website.

Clicking "continue" brings you to the editor. This is the default embedded form.

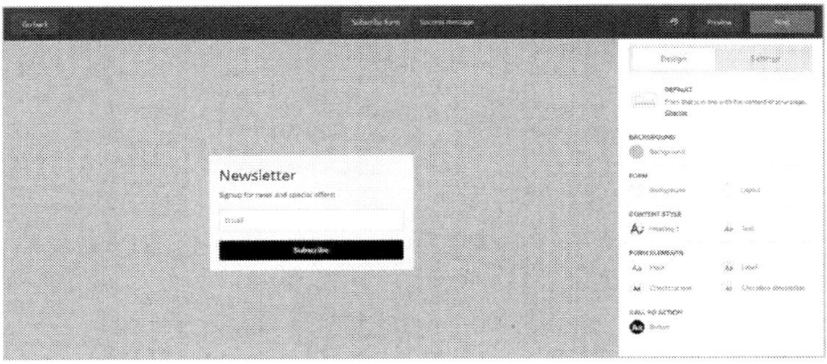

Told you it was simplistic! This only allows you to vary the font: there are no pictures, no other content. So, adjust your words on your form, add a reCAPTCHA code if you wish (from the Settings panel), and the other form set-up activities we did for the landing page, but without the added detail of a picture because, presumably, that picture is already the banner on your website so you don't need it a second time.

(Aside: if you really, REALLY, want a picture on your embedded form, click "Change" in the Design panel under DEFAULT. This gives you other options for the layout. The third option, CARD, includes a picture.)

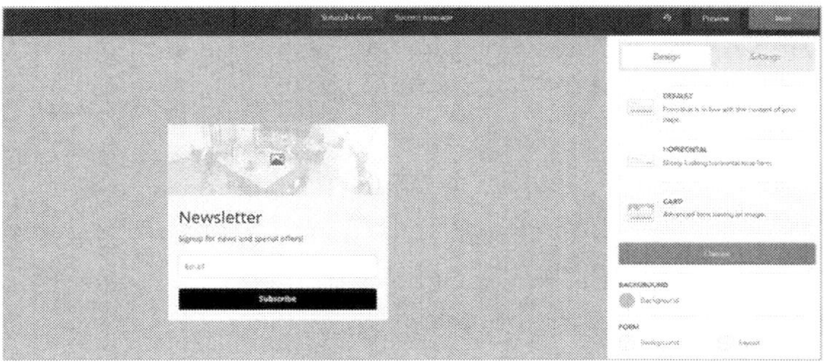

One thing to consider in the colors is that you want them to pop on your website. The colors that might suit your landing page, which has a full screen to itself, may not work for a form that needs to stand out on a standard webpage. If you have a dark background on your website (gray, navy, or black, for example) perhaps a strong bright color – white, yellow, orange even – would pop. If you have white as your background, a strong primary color would stand out. If you are using a strong primary color as your background, make sure you have a contrast for your form – white can often work well in this case. Play around with the colors and find a design that works for you.

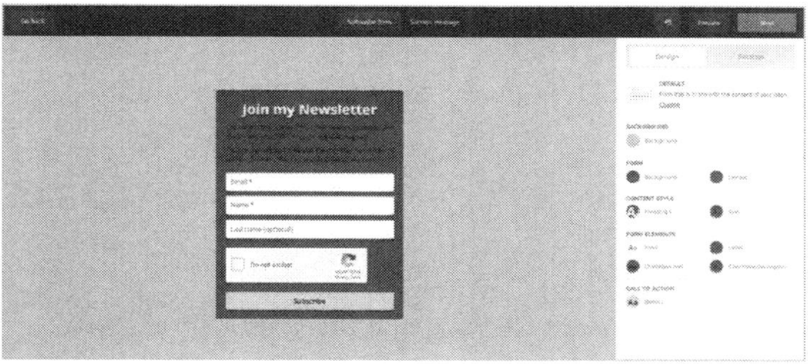

Once you have your subscribe form complete, you need to create a **Success message**. This will appear in the same "box" as your embedded form, after the subscriber has successfully submitted their details. Like with the success form for the landing page, you need to remind them of the need to check for their confirmation email and to whitelist your address. Similar wording can be applied but remember the different dimensions and color palette that you'll have to work with (the Success message follows the same colors as you set up for the Subscribe form).

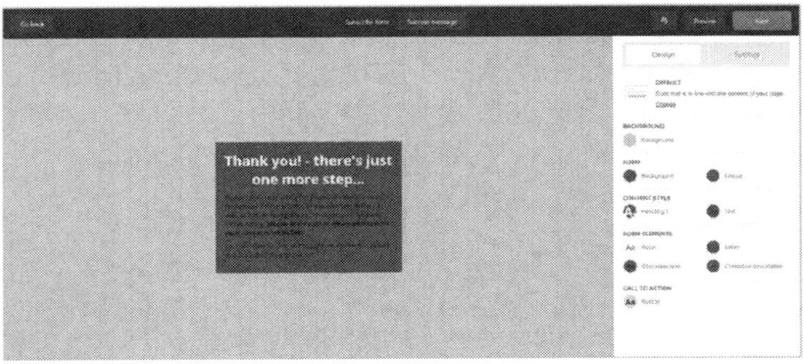

When you have finished editing your Subscriber form and Success message, click the green **Next** button in the top right corner. This brings you to the Overview page for the embedded form. As with the landing page set-up, ensure Double opt-in is switched on. The Double Opt-In email and associated Thank you page can be customized in the same manner as already discussed for the landing page.

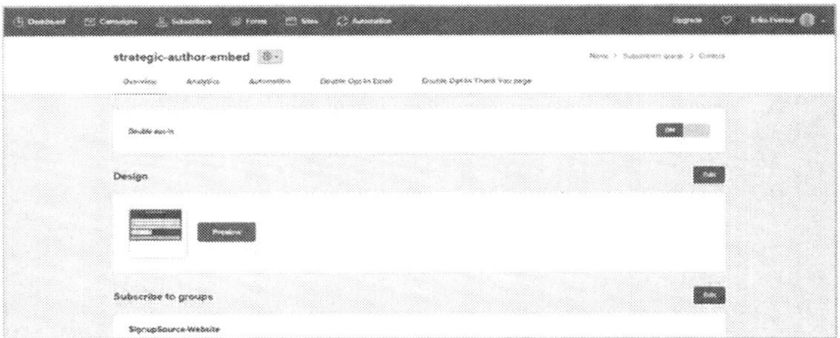

Scrolling to the bottom of the Overview page, you will see options for how to **Embed form into your website**. One method is to copy the given HTML code and insert it into your HTML editor on your website in the desired spot. Another is based on adding a Java script to each page of your website. Whichever you choose, MailerLite gives instructions on how/where to use each piece of code, and the code has all your customization choices already specified in the code.

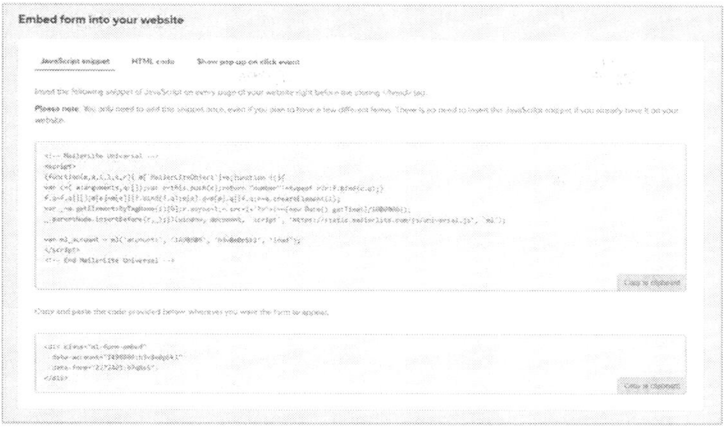

How your website is set up and how you integrate the code generated by MailerLite with your website is outside the scope of this book, as I said before. But accessing HTML or Javascript editors should be explained in tutorials for your web-builder, which may help with this.

8.4. Updating subscriber profiles

There may be personalized information you wish to collect about your subscribers beyond their names, to engage them in additional ways. One example is a birthday so that you can send them a birthday email and wish them a happy day.

Asking for extra information at sign-up is going to lead to fewer people being willing to sign up. As mentioned before, you want to keep the sign-up process as simple as possible. To get around this, you can invite a subscriber to update their profile in your database *after* they have joined your list. This is a little bit trickier than just getting information at the start. But it finds a balance between minimizing the burden at sign-up and maximizing the collection of information, by asking for the additional information later, when they feel more comfortable giving it to you.

8.4.1. Creating a custom field

The first step is to create a new custom field to store the information you want. Go to **Subscribers** (on the green ribbon) and select **Fields** within that. Click the orange **Add new field** button to create a new field.

A pop-up box will appear asking you for the name you want to assign to the new field and what type of variable it is. There are three 'types' of variables: Text, Number, and Date.

For example, to collect a birthday, create a new field called birthday and set it as a date field. When you click the Create button, you will revert to the screen with the list of Fields, and your new field will be at the bottom of the list.

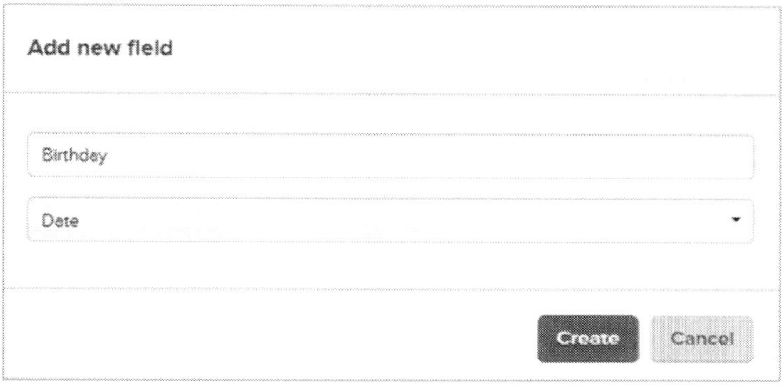

8.4.2. Populating a custom field

To allow subscribers to update a field on their profile, you need to create a new landing page. On this landing page, you will have email and whatever fields you want them to update. The subscriber will need to enter the *same* email address they used to sign up to your list initially, and this needs to be made clear.

Date fields like Birthday are collected as year-month-day (yyyy-mm-dd). There is no way to collect day and month without also collecting the year. (Well, you could collect it as a Text variable, but then MailerLite wouldn't be able to recognize the entry as a date so couldn't trigger emails based on the date. This defeats the purpose of collecting birthdays, so you need this field to be a date.)

Age and year of birth can be sensitive information for some people. To balance privacy with collecting information in a useful format, subscribers can enter 1900 as the year of birth as a way of saying "none of your business" and you should inform them of this option on the sign-up form.

The associated Success page for this birthday landing page can be a simple message: Thank you, your birthday has been recorded.

You don't need to double opt-in for *this* landing page, because the subscribers are already on your list (and have confirmed that they want to be.) This is just a way to update information for existing subscribers.

To invite your readers to provide this information, include the link to this landing page in an email to your mailing list. A good time to ask for this could be at the end of your onboarding sequence when you have had the chance to 'warm them up' and they have decided they want to stick around to hear more from you.

9. Campaign stats / assessing engagement

Chapter Objectives

- *Knowing how to assess the performance (engagement) of each email you send.*
- *Using split testing to improve engagement on your emails.*
- *Identifying and removing subscribers with low engagement.*

On the dashboard, you can see stats for your last campaign (email) sent.

The numbers shown here represent the reach of your emails and your subscribers' engagement with them. The first number is the number of email recipients i.e. the number of subscribers this email has been sent to. The second number is the percentage of recipients who opened the email and the third is the percentage of recipients who clicked a link in that email. If you hover your cursor over the percentages, the actual *number* of recipients who have opened/clicked that email will be displayed.

A high click percentage means people are directly engaging with your content, that they will follow a link if you provide one. Most email providers see click percentage as a very valuable metric to gauge whether you are engaging your audience. However, as authors, we're trying to maintain a balance between the give-ask ratio, so we won't be asking for clicks in every email. Therefore, you may have emails with low click percentages only because you have not included a link to ask for clicks. These emails with no clicks will also affect the average clicks across your history. Bear this in mind when you're assessing those stats and put them in context for yourself.

The **Dashboard** only shows the stats for your most recent campaign. To see the stats for all your email campaigns, go to the **Campaign** tab and select 'sent' emails. if you want to see how your onboarding sequence is working (or, indeed, any other automation workflow) go to the **Automation** section. Open the 'overview' for the workflow of interest. At the bottom of the overview page, you will see a similar set of stats for each of the emails in the workflow. This can help you understand where in your automation sequence you might be having at drop off in attention span (i.e. engagement), as another way of identifying what your readers are interested in hearing about. If you see a lack of engagement and can't work out why, and want to increase those numbers, then you may want to try a split test campaign to look at different presentation options to the same audience to see what resonates best. I'll talk about this in the next section.

Each year in their annual report, MailerLite publishes the average open and click rates for emails overall for everyone on their platform, and also broken down by industry. The average rates in 2019 across all industries were:

The 2019 email marketing benchmarks

23,65%	3,55%	0,32%	0,63%
Open rate	Click rate	Unsubscribe rate	Bounce rate

"Authors" are not listed as an individual industry, but here are five adjacent industries that authors would be comparable to (I don't know in which category MailerLite includes account holders who identify as 'authors' in their registration.)

Industry	Open rate	Click rate	Unsubscribe rate	Bounce rate
Arts and artists	24.38%	4.03%	0.35%	0.32%
Creative services and agency	24.19%	3.66%	0.36%	0.37%
Education and training	25.46%	3.94%	0.28%	0.45%
Entertainment and events	18.17%	2.62%	0.23%	0.26%
Media and publishing	22.82%	4.33%	0.24%	0.26%
	23.00%	3.72%	0.29%	0.33%

You can see that the average reported by MailerLite for these five categories is a 23% open rate and a 3.7% click rate. Building a strong connection with your readers through your email platform means that you should be able to achieve numbers much higher than this. If your open rates are north of 50% you're doing well, particularly if you have built your newsletter through promotions. If your newsletter is organic only (people who have signed up for your list only after reading your books) you want this number to be possibly north of 70% for opens. As I said before, the number of clicks is very dependent on how often you ask people to click, so look at the click rates in those 'ask' emails separately rather than at your overall average across all emails.

One way to improve your percentages is to prune your list regularly. Pruning means removing people who are not engaging with your emails from your mailing list, and this is discussed further in Section 9.2. Unlike split testing, pruning your list won't improve the *number* of people engaging with your content. I still see it as valuable though, as improving the *percentages* can help your overall sender reputation which may in turn help more people to see your emails (because they will be 'relevant' so they won't be diverted to spam folders.)

9.1. Split testing aka A/B testing

Split testing allows you to change one element of an email to see whether that change will resonate better with your audience. There are 3 aspects of your email that you can change with split testing:

- the subject line,
- the sender, and
- the email content.

You can only change one of these elements at a time, and the two resulting versions are called Option A and Option B. This screenshot shows a selection for testing different subject lines, and how each option is identified as A or B.

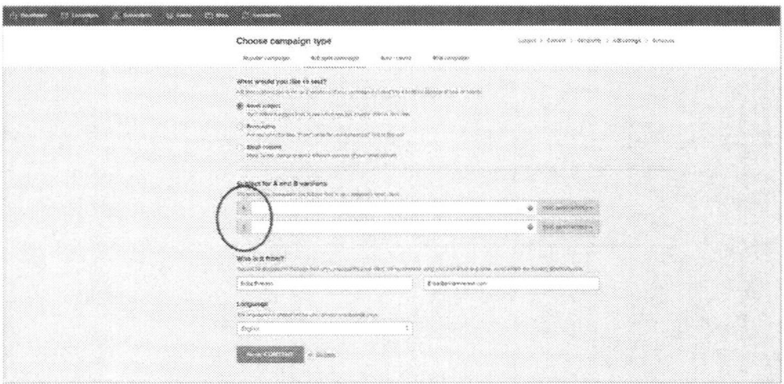

Split testing sends Option A to a fraction of your subscriber list, Option B to another fraction of your email list of the same size, and then the option that has the most engagement will be sent to the rest of your email list. For example, option A goes to 20% of your list, option B goes to another 20% of your list, and then the remaining 60% will get whichever option performs better between A and B. This gives you information about what your readers like and respond to, and also ensures that most people are getting the email that will resonate best with them. You can adjust the fractions for the test groups and remaining recipients when setting up your split test, during the **A/B Settings** step of the setup.

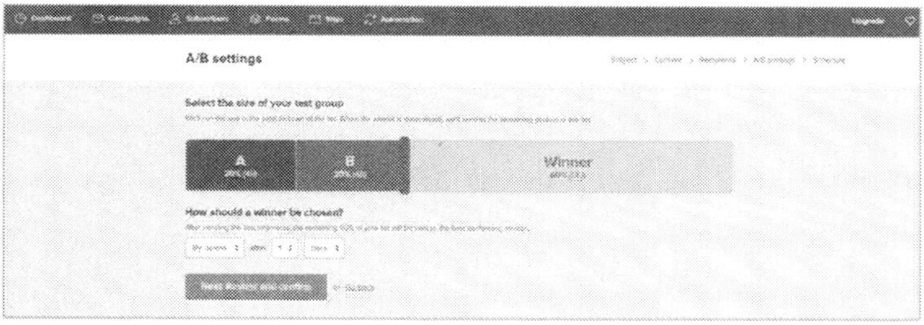

There are different criteria for success that you can set. You specify these in the **How should a winner be chosen?** section after adjusting the sizes of the test groups. You can define success as the email that gets the highest number of **opens** or the highest number of **clicks** (on any links within the mail) between Option A and Option B.

You have to set a time limit after which the winning option will be identified. This time limit is important in that you need to allow your test readers a chance to take action or not, but also you don't want a campaign to wait too long to send to the remainder of your list. You can set the assessment time in either hours or days. The 'right' choice depends on many factors only you can determine, such as the usual frequency of your emails, how quickly your readers typically open your emails, the time-sensitivity of the email (to be sent to the remainder of the list), etc.

9.2. Maintaining your subscriber list

Chapter Objectives

- *Defining what constitutes a non-engaged subscriber for your newsletter.*
- *Using manual and MailerLite's automatic methods to identify these non-engaged subscribers.*
- *Setting up an automated workflow to ensure the identified subscribers are truly non-engaged.*
- *Removing the (confirmed) non-engaged subscribers from your mailing list.*

9.2.1. Identifying non-engaged subscribers

In the Subscribers tab (on the green ribbon), there is an option to **Clean up inactive**. This is a MailerLite default. It defines inactive subscribers as those who have been on your list for more than 6 months but haven't open to any of your emails. These are unquestionably dead weight and should be removed. MailerLite makes this simple: the big orange **Unsubscribe inactive** button at the top means you can clear out all of the inactive subscribers they have identified with one click.

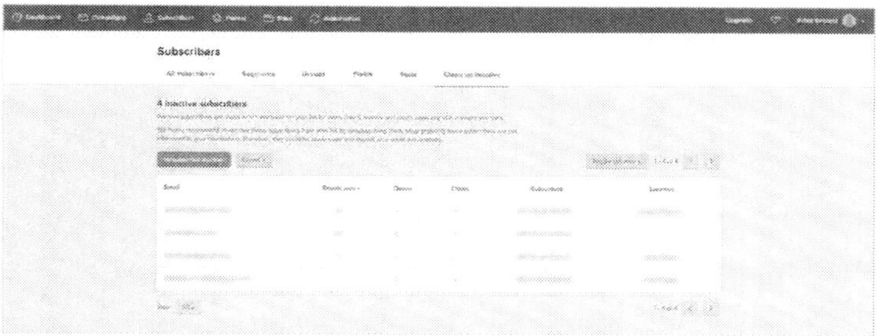

However, you may have more stringent criteria for what you consider an active subscriber. If you go to the **All subscribers** list, you'll see an option to choose a filter among your active subscribers. Within that select "time inactive" (the second-last option) and you can define that as they have not opened or clicked any email in the last X days. MailerLite presents 5 days as the default, but that value can be whatever you feel is appropriate. So, if you're sending emails frequently, it might be a month. If you only send an email once a month, maybe it's for your last 3 campaigns which would be a 90-day window. It's entirely up to you as to what you feel constitutes *engaged* in your process.

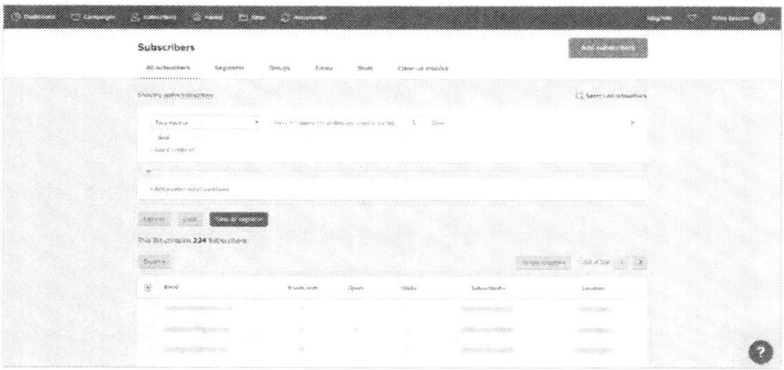

By selecting this subset, you can then save these people as a segment or as a group and in doing so you can deal with them to manage them out of your list. **Save as segment** is obvious because it is a green button on the screen, but it is not your only option. Select the subset by clicking the arrow button at the top of the 'tick box' column and choose "select all." When you do this, a yellow banner will appear to confirm how many subscribers you have selected, and a new option **Actions** will appear above the list.

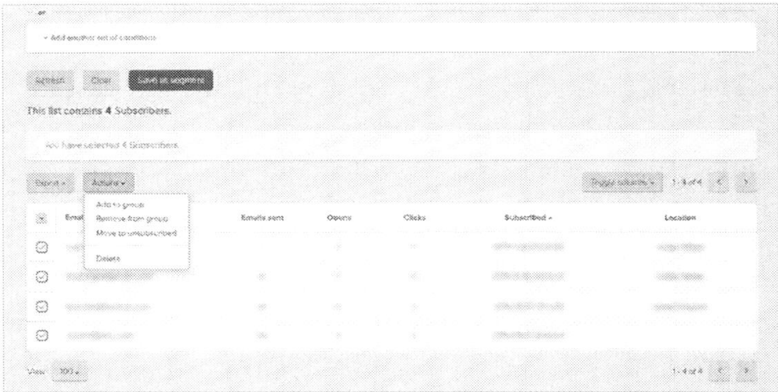

As you can see, the third option is to "Move to unsubscribed" but this will immediately remove them from your list. It may be that these people have been opening your emails in a preview pane, so it's not registering for MailerLite that they have been reading. Therefore, I would suggest launching a re-engagement campaign, to confirm that they really do want to be removed from the list. A lack of response can be considered as confirmation of that. Then, they can tell you if they wish to stay, so you don't lose someone who is actually engaged, even if they don't appear to be.

Another option for identifying inactive subscribers is to select specific emails that they have or have not received, opened, or clicked. Using the filter **Campaigns**, you can specify exactly which campaigns (emails) you want to be included in this. However, you will have to select each email separately (from the drop-down list of emails in "Any Campaign" below).

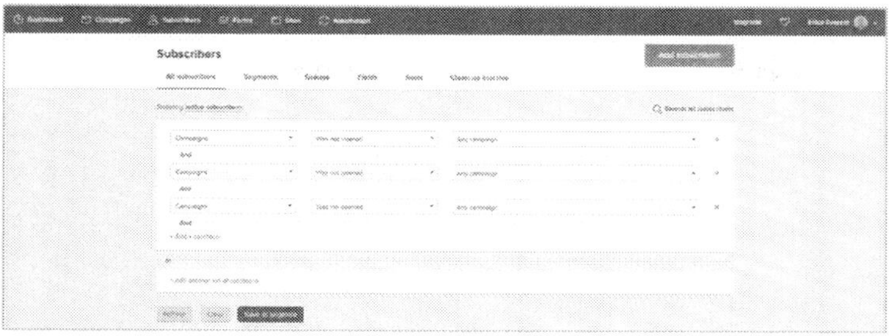

If you send on a regular schedule it is probably easier to select the timeframe rather than having to pick out the most recent X emails to determine whether someone is actively engaged. The condition based on time is also easily repeatable at regular intervals.

However you define inactive, add the subscribers identified via this process to a group called UNENGAGED, and start a re-engagement campaign to confirm whether they will stay or go.

9.2.2. Re-engagement campaigns

Once you've identified your unengaged subscribers and added them to the group UNENGAGED, create a workflow (automation sequence) to assess what to do with them next. Set up a series of three emails, each a variation on the same thing.

The first email tells them that they have been identified as unengaged and why. Don't necessarily use that word – maybe something along the lines of "according to my records you not opened any email from me since May 1st," and then ask them if they still want to hear from you or if they'd like to be removed from your list. Give them a button to reply to confirm that they wish to remain, and tell them that if they do not reply they will be automatically removed in two weeks.

A week later, send the second email saying much the same thing, but reminding them that the countdown is now only one week. Finally, send the final email 24-48 hours before the removal deadline, depending on how much notice you want to give them for this final approach.

Before sending emails 2 and 3 in the sequence, do a check to confirm they haven't clicked on the "engaged" button, in which case they should be removed from this workflow and moved from the UNENGAGED group to the REGULAR group. If they have ignored all emails or otherwise confirmed that they no longer wish to be on your subscriber list, tag them as UNSUBSCRIBED and then send them your standard unsubscribe email. This email

- confirms that they have been removed from your list,
- gives them a link to rejoin with, if they change their mind, and
- informs them that if they wish to know about your future new releases that they can follow you on Amazon or BookBub (provide links to both platforms to make it easy for them.)

The final step is to delete them from your active list.

And you're done.

9.2.3. Pruning the list

Even when you send someone to the UNSUBSCRIBE list, and remove them from your active campaigns, MailerLite will still consider them an active subscriber for 30 days after the last email you sent to them. This is important because as you reach your 1000 subscriber limit for the free plan, you might do a purge then immediately wish to incorporate some new subscribers, but you won't be able to do that because of the lag time.

You can wait 30 days to import those new subscribers or you can manage your list a little more cleverly. I would advise you to regularly run your search for unengaged subscribers and put them through this sequence to remove them from your list. In particular, running it at least a month before any big promotion or book release is important. That way, they will already have cleared your active list by the time new subscribers start to join and you want to send emails to them, without affecting your upper limit.

Mainly we've been discussing this at the threshold between free and paid at 1000 subscribers, but of course, there are other thresholds for price increases based on the number of subscribers. The same principles for maintaining and pruning your subscriber list apply there too.

10. In conclusion

If you are one of those people who implements advice as you read it, congratulations – you have just built an onboarding sequence to funnel subscribers from sign-up onto your mailing list, and generated compelling content newsletters to keep them there!

If you are like me and like to read a book through first before you tackle implementing any of it, you may be feeling a bit overwhelmed. Firstly, take a deep breath. Secondly, thank you for reading this far! To help you navigate through the book again, here is an overview of the key sections and how to use them.

Start with Chapter 2 to get your MailerLite account set up and approved, with all the other requirements that need to be in place to get that approval. (If you don't already have a MailerLite account, here is an affiliate MailerLite sign-up link, which gives *you* $20 credit on sign-up and me credit if you later upgrade to a paid plan – at no extra cost to you. https://www.mailerlite.com/invite/7421128630ec5)

Consider what content you want to include in your regular newsletters (Section 6.2), create an author brand image (Section 2.5), and use these to build an email template as described in Chapter 3.

If you don't already have a reader magnet, write one, and set up a distribution link for it on BookFunnel (or equivalent platform) as described in Chapter 5.

Write the content of your onboarding sequence emails, using the prompts in Section 6.1.

Use the workflow layout described in Chapter 7 (particularly in the final image) to build your onboarding sequence, using the workflow elements described in Chapter 4. Combine the content of your onboarding emails from Section 6.1 with the email template from Chapter 3, to create the emails for your workflow.

Pro Tip: think about what images you want to use across all of your onboarding emails, and your author branding. If you cannot get a bundle deal (e.g. 100 images for $100 with no expiry on Deposit Photos) you can use their flexible monthly plan instead. This is $30 per month for up to 30 images – if you know what images you want in advance, you can use one month's membership to get all the images you need, at an average cost of $1 an image. And then cancel your subscription when you have the images you need. (This is acceptable at the time of writing, but check terms of service before joining any subscription service, in case there are changes in future.)

Now that you have an onboarding sequence set up, you are ready to accept subscribers. Build sign-up pages or forms as outlined in Chapter 8, and then share these links to attract subscribers to your mailing list.

Set a reminder to check the "health" of your mailing list at regular intervals. Test changes to improve engagement and cull subscribers who are not engaged. Following the steps in Chapter 9 will ensure you don't pay for dead-weight subscribers and that your open and click rates contribute to a positive sender reputation.

I hope this guide helps you to be more strategic in how you build and leverage your author newsletter, by minimizing your time spend while maximizing your engagement rates. Best of luck!

11. Recommended resources

Newsletter Ninja: How to Become an Author Mailing List Expert by Tammi Labrecque www.amazon.com/dp/B07C6J8HP9

Strangers to Superfans: A Marketing Guide to The Reader Journey by David Gaughran www.amazon.com/dp/B0798PH9QT

Reader Magnets: Build Your Author Platform and Sell more Books on Kindle (2019 Edition) by Nick Stephenson www.amazon.com/dp/B00PCKIJ4C

CAN-SPAM Act (2003): https://www.ftc.gov/tips-advice/business-center/guidance/can-spam-act-compliance-guide-business

EU e-Privacy Directive (2002): https://eur-lex.europa.eu/LexUriServ/LexUriServ.do?uri=CELEX:32002L0058:EN:HTML

MailerLite sign up link: https://www.mailerlite.com/invite/7421128630ec5 (note this is an affiliate link)

BookFunnel sign up link https://bookfunnel.com/

MailerLite engagement benchmarks 2019
https://www.mailerlite.com/blog/compare-your-email-performance-metrics-industry-benchmarks

Author Notes

Firstly, a huge thank you to you, the reader, for not only reading the whole book but also reading these author notes as well. This book has been a labor of love for me, and I hope you found it useful.

I couldn't have done this alone, however. I need to say a massive thank you to Fatima, Elaine, Robyn, Kasia, and Anne – the Beta testers who were with me every step of the way, encouraging me to put this book together in the first place, then testing the strategies I proposed, and providing feedback when something wasn't clear. Ladies, you are amazing. Thank you from the bottom of my heart

I'd also like to thank my extraordinary proofreading team – James, Julian, and Robyn – who diligently checked every word, every cross-reference, to ensure the cleanest manuscript possible. Any errors remaining are entirely my own fault. If you find any, please let me know via the contact form on my website at http://erikaeverest.com/Strategic-Author.php.

The *Strategic Author Series* is based on taking a strategic approach to how you spend your time and money. This book is not meant to be a definitive guide or the one true way to use MailerLite or build newsletters. There are many ways to define success and many ways to achieve that success – and success with mailing lists is no different. There may be things you want to explore not covered here, or you may have a different experience with the structure I have proposed. Whatever your feedback, I'd love to hear it! You can reach me via the link above.

Erika Everest

1st August 2020

Printed in Great Britain
by Amazon

29494322R00082